8/10/13

Remember you were made for love,

MADE FOR LOVE

Thoughts from the Watering Hole of Love, Grace, and African Tales

EDSON L. KNAPP

CROSSBOOKS

CrossBooks™
A Division of LifeWay
1663 Liberty Drive
Bloomington, IN 47403
www.crossbooks.com
Phone: 1-866-879-0502

First published by CrossBooks 06/29/2012

ISBN: 978-1-4627-1427-8 (sc)
ISBN: 978-1-4627-1429-2 (hc)
ISBN: 978-1-4627-1428-5 (e)

Library of Congress Control Number: 2012902673

Printed in the United States of America

This book is printed on acid-free paper.

Praise Leaps

The hippos were leaping today, Lord,
    Leaping,
        Like frisky horses or calves,
            Bounding out of the water.
The crocodiles slithered along
    With only their eyes to give
        Their presence away.
The egrets flapped in unison
    As they went to roost.
The sky was a gray-pink washboard
    With a mound of gray clothes
        Waiting to be washed on it.
The spoonbills hurried along,
    Scooping dessert before darkness
        Ended their meal.
The elephants wanted a quick bath
    Before their dinner.
The bee eaters, en masse, swept out
    Of their high rise, cliff apartments.
And I could only watch in awe
    As each creation seemed to be
        Praising You, Lord
            Just by doing what You created it to do.

                            – Suzanne Knapp Groce

PREFACE

My mother traveled three hours on muddy potholed roads to reach the hospital where I was born. It was a small mission hospital in Mbeya, Tanzania. I was raised, the son of missionaries, in a small rural district in southern Tanzania. My life was filled with farming, dust, tropical rainstorms, and God. From my parents I learned about a God who loves me.

Many an hour I spent in my room during an afternoon thunderstorm, reading a book and listening to the rain fall from our thatched roof onto the trees and bushes outside my room. In those quiet times, I learned of a God who loves me.

Now I am married and live in Tennessee. I have seven children, one adopted from Ethiopia. My wife and I are doctors. She is an obstetrician, and I am a radiologist. This book came out of my desire to share some of the stories of African life and my life as a father of seven. We have had so many fun and scary times with God. He sustains us and keeps us and loves us.

I came to realize a few years ago that God's love and grace was meant for me. I don't mean that I was unique. I realized that God makes each one of us for love and grace. We are made for love. We are made for grace. So, share with me some stories from Africa and elsewhere. Share with me love, grace, and African tales.

DEDICATION

To my wife, Renda. She is the smartest, most beautiful person I know. More importantly, she walks after God—and I am the one who benefits. This book has only happened because of her encouragement, advice, and editing. I am and will be always grateful for the woman God has given me to be my wife.

To my parents, for without their willingness to go to Tanzania, these stories would never have happened. My father's soft heart has always led me to remember the mercy of God. My mother's fierce perseverance in the face of impossible circumstances reminds me daily that much can be accomplished by the obedient who keep saying yes to God's will.

To my children who love me more than a dad deserves. This book contains many of the stories they love to hear at home around the dinner table.

To my pastors, Allen Jessee and Craig Barber, who taught me and encouraged me and became my friends through their gracious kindness to a displaced missionary kid.

DAY 1

Grace through Christ

For the Law was given through Moses; grace and truth were realized through Jesus Christ.

John 1:17

Grace

The dirty, dusty, bumpy roads were a fixture on Sunday evenings. After a long day of church, communion, and a baptismal service, we all crammed into the Land Rover and drove for an hour or two or three to arrive home Sunday evening, exhausted. I was always packed like a sardine into the back of the vehicle with friendly but very smelly church members who needed a ride home. Somewhere between the bumps, a voice would start a song, and we would all join in. Depending on who was with us, the songs would either have layers of harmony or just be off key. We didn't care. The singing passed the time and took our minds off the smell and onto the fun of the songs. One of our favorites went, "When we all get to heaven we will have ..." After the word *have,* we would list the things we wished heaven would provide. The most popular choice was streets of gold. We grew so tired of the bumpy roads that we would dream of streets of gold.

On one long trip back, my friend Diki added a new wish: "When we all get to heaven we will have meat and gravy." We laughed and sang about wanting meat and gravy in heaven. We sang at the top of our voices. We laughed because Diki never had enough to eat; he was always hungry. He probably had a tapeworm.

When I think of good times, times of joy, I think about what was given to us through Jesus Christ. The gift of grace from truth comes from Him. All the joy and all the happiness we have come from Him. The good times are His gift. Before we knew Him, when we despised Him, He planned good for us. He planned laughter and memories and happiness. He gives grace and truth.

Question

Do I choose His grace and truth, or do I spend my days in pettiness and grumbling? Am I using the time He gives embracing the life He has given, or am I resentful of my past failures? Am I locked in memories or worried about the future? Shouldn't I be living in today, loving Him and His people?

Pray

Father, teach me to live in Your grace and Your truth. Help me to stop worrying about my past and my future. Give me a passion for You. Give me your daily grace.

DAY 2

The Love of Christ

"You have heard that it was said, 'You shall love your neighbor and hate your enemy.' But I say to you, love your enemies and pray for those who persecute you, so that you may be sons of your Father who is in heaven."

Matthew 5:43–45

The African Darkness

When Dad first began his work in Tanzania, he started a farm. He used the farm to demonstrate new crops and techniques to help the local farmers. However, the tribesmen were afraid of him. If we went to visit them, they would run away. If we met them on the paths, they would run into the jungle. When we tried to talk to them, they would run away. But farmers want better crops, and as they watched Dad's corn grow with multiple ears (much more than the local corn), they became curious. Dad decided to leave seed packets on the fence posts on the edge of our property. All the seed packets disappeared. He left more packets, and these also disappeared. Then the farmers would let Dad talk to them from across fields. He gradually taught them trust until they would let him approach and teach them about the new crops he had brought to share with them. Later, we found out that the local witchdoctor had told everyone that the white man had come to steal the blood of the Africans. The white man, he said, used black men's blood to make cars and other extraordinary things the white man had. The witchdoctor told them Dad had come to kill their children for blood.

When Mom and Dad retired from their work more than twenty years later, they reminded their friends of those days long ago when the people were afraid. An older man who had become a Christian near the beginning of their ministry rose and said, "Bwana Knapp, when you came, we were in darkness. You brought us the light of Christ. Now we are no longer afraid."

Question

When others are afraid of Christ's love, how do I react? Do I pray for those who persecute me? Do I turn the other cheek? Do I share the love He shared with me? Do I bring light where once there was darkness?

Pray

I want to share Your love with my enemies. Help me to pray for those who hate me. When I am betrayed, give me forgiveness for them, for they know not what they do. Give me love for the fallen. Give me your compassion.

DAY 3

Created by Love to Live

Though you have not seen Him, you love Him, and though you do not see Him now, but believe in Him, you greatly rejoice with joy inexpressible and full of glory, obtaining as the outcome of your faith the salvation of your souls.

1 Peter 1:8-9

Pots

Near where I grew up in Southern Tanzania, there is a small peninsula called Ikombe, which juts out from the rugged Livingstone Mountains into Lake Nyasa. Living in this small village is the Kisi tribe, known for making pots. Their pots are used by people all over Tanzania. The pots are popular because they are waterproof, light, and strong. They are made from a light white clay gathered from the base of the mountain range on this small peninsula.

I remember visiting Ikombe when I was young. To get there, we had to travel by canoe. When we arrived at Ikombe, we walked through the village, noticing that there were women sitting outside each house, making their pots. Each pot began as a ball of unformed clay. The women hollowed them out, often using a corncob to help form the shape. With their left hand, they turned the pot, and with their right, they created the shape. After the pot dried for several days, it would be decorated with a red ochre clay and then fired. Each pot was made for a specific purpose: some to hold water in a home, others for cooking rice, and others for decoration.

God, the pot maker, is our maker. He has crafted each one of us uniquely. He has crafted us to love. This yearning we have for God and for each other comes from His making. We love Him, believe in Him, and rejoice with Him because we were made for love by Love. That is why God commands us to love Him, because He made us—crafted us—to love Him.

Question

Am I using what He crafted for the purpose for which it was made?

Pray

Father, help me to be what You made me. Forgive me for choosing myself over You. Help me to choose obedience to Your word. Fill me with Your joy and holiness. Fill me with true life.

DAY 4

The Humble

But He gives a greater grace. Therefore it says, "God is opposed to the proud, but gives grace to the humble."

James 4:6

A Soft Heart

He sat in the yard, listening to stories. The stories were similar, all tales of woe and poverty. "If we only had money, we could get medical care for our sick child," or "Just a little money would help us finish our roof." Some of the storytellers were repeat offenders. They had borrowed money before, but they had not repaid their last loan. Now they were back for another handout. He patiently listened while they explained some new problem that had beset them. These conversations took up so much time. He never complained. He listened and advised, and most of all, he listened with humility. Whenever he could, he would help. There was no timetable for repayment, no list or record to keep account.

When asked why he was so generous, he replied, "Because they need help. How would I look before my Master, who forgave my debt, if I did not help them as I am able?"

Over the years, it seemed everyone knew someone who had received help in one form or another from him. He taught them how to farm better, how to feed their families, how to raise crops they could sell to make a little money.

Now in his eighties, he cares for his wife, whose health is less than his own. He no longer directs a large district of four hundred churches. He no longer preaches every Sunday morning and night, a farmer who used to be in more demand than most pastors.

The Africans used to tell you if you asked, "Bwana Nepu, he has a soft heart," by which they meant that he was humble, always placing himself to serve others. I realize God has given my dad greater grace.

Question

Am I humble? Do I consider the needs of others greater than myself? Do I know I am here at His calling? All that I am is from His hand. Do I acknowledge that He has given what and who I am?

Pray

Father, give me Your greater grace. Teach me humbleness and from that humility. Pass Your grace to those around me who need You.

DAY 5

Pineapple

I shall delight in Your commandments, which I love. And I shall lift up my hands to Your commandments, which I love; and I will meditate on Your statutes.

Psalm 119:47–48

Breakfast

As a child, nearly every morning I ate fresh pineapple from our farm. They were the ripest, biggest pineapples you could imagine. Full of sweet juice, gushing into your mouth with every bite. You could eat as much as you wanted every morning. The plants were imported from Hawaii, and they flourished in our tropical Tanzanian climate. I loved pineapple.

Loving His Commandments

David loved God's word in the same way that I loved pineapple as a child. He wrote about God's word. He studied and memorized and meditated on it. He told others about it. Now, if you try to read through Leviticus, by chapter five, you will begin to wonder if David was right in the head. But I have discovered that David did not delight in genealogies or how many chapters he read per day. Instead, David delighted in his relationship with God. That relationship grew from learning about God from His word. His commandments, His instruction, His laws teach us about God and who He is. It is from those laws that we learn how He wants us to treat our neighbors, how He wants us to love one another, and how He wants us to love Him. As we meditate on these things of God, His Spirit fills us with pleasure. It is the holy pleasure of knowing God.

Question

Is God someone you hear about on Sunday morning when you are dressed up? Or is He a vital part of every moment? Do you talk with Him on Sundays or every waking moment? Do you delight in His word in the same way I delighted in pineapple when I was a child?

Pray

Teach me to pray without ceasing. Teach me to fill every moment with Your presence. Let my day be filled with Your light radiating from me, lighting the lives of others crossing my path.

DAY 6

The Excellence of Love

Love is patient, love is kind, and is not jealous; love does not brag and is not arrogant, does not act unbecomingly; it does not seek its own, is not provoked, does not take into account a wrong suffered, does not rejoice in unrighteousness, but rejoices with the truth; bears all things, believes all things, hopes all things, endures all things.

1 Corinthians 13:4-7

A Quiet Life

He was one of the first people who accepted Christ when my parents moved to Kyela. His name was George Moses. As he grew in his faith, he became a pastor. He was a gentle man, and I remember going to his home and eating with his family. My favorite food was chicken and rice. The chicken was cooked in palm oil (not very healthy but wow!). I could eat a ton of that food. The rice in Kyela has its own special flavor—better than any other rice in the world. I thought it was odd that he served the food with his youngest daughter; his wife did not help. I learned when I was a little older that his wife had some health problems, and she did not cook or work their farm.

In that culture, a woman like that would normally be put away (divorced), and the man would marry again, maybe multiple wives. No self-respecting man there would put up with a woman who couldn't tend the farm and cook and raise the children. Pastor Moses was different. He knew the Scriptures. Only one wife and only one marriage. I never heard him complain about his life. No one ever heard him complain.

Faithfulness describes George Moses and his life. When I read I Corinthians chapter 13, I think of George Moses. I think of a man who spent his life choosing kindness and patience. Humbleness and endurance were choices he made for love, a quiet love illustrated by his life.

Question

How patient am I? How kind, humble, forgiving, enduring am I? God commands love. Do I seek good for others instead of myself?

Pray

Father, give me Your love, the kind of love that seeks righteousness for others and believes with hope. Replace my arrogance with Your humility. Give me Your patience and Your truth.

DAY 7

Abounding Grace

The Law came in so that the transgression would increase; but where sin increased, grace abounded all the more, so that, as sin reigned in death, even so grace would reign through righteousness to eternal life through Jesus Christ our Lord.

Romans 5:20-21

Waterfalls

On hot, dusty, summer days you need something to do with your friends. So Safe and Peteli and I, along with anyone else interested, would walk from our farm up to the Livingstone Mountains. Along the way, we passed fields of pineapples on our farm. We waded across the Mwalisi River and onto the government sugarcane farm. We walked in bare feet, one little white boy and a lot of little Africans. It was a strange sight except to us. After sugarcane fields, we wandered through woodlands and brush. Sometimes we saw monkeys playing or guinea fowl rustling. After an hour or so, we came to a stunning waterfall. It was where the Mwalisi River fell to the foot of the Livingstone Mountains and entered the plains. The falls had carved a large oval amphitheater out of solid rock with a pool about twenty feet deep. When the rains fell, the whole oval chamber was filled with water, but in the summer the falls filled only the back of the pool, and we could swim to our hearts' content. The water was crystal clear, filtered by layers of rock and a three thousand foot drop from the mountains above. Along the left wall, there were just enough cuts in the rock to climb the edge and jump in from about fifteen feet. We played to exhaustion and played some more. The only sad part was when the sun neared the western horizon; we would climb out and return down the slopes, reaching home as dusk settled across the valley.

I think God's abounding grace is like that waterfall. There is more than anyone could ever need. It heals and washes and cleans us from our dry, hopeless selves. All the dust of this world is washed away. God gives grace, pouring it out into our lives, flowing from us to others. It is His abounding grace.

Question

Am I letting God's grace flow fully into my life? Do I try to limit His waterfall of grace, trying to turn it into a water fountain?

Pray

Father, thank You for Your abounding grace. Help me to open my heart to grace, not holding back from the adventure You have planned for me. Teach me to trust You, to trust Your heart instead of trusting my fears. King of Kings, I bow before Your throne of majesty, Your heart of love, Your gift of abounding grace.

DAY 8

Adventure

God has not given us a spirit of timidity, but of power and love and discipline. Therefore do not be ashamed of the testimony of our Lord, or of me His prisoner, but join with me in suffering for the gospel according to the power of God, who has saved us and called us with a holy calling.

2 Timothy 1:7-9

Birthday

It was Sunday. It was raining when we awoke. Our Land Rover was broken, and we only had the Volkswagen Beetle to drive. Dad had been asked to preach at a church that was about an hour and a half drive from where we lived. Mom was sick, so he decided to go alone. Mom was worried about the roads, but Dad told her that because it was her birthday, many people in the United States were praying for them. Little did he know the adventure ahead.

He arrived home after dusk. Dad was muddy. He came into the house exhausted and told us his story. "When I left, the rain was not too bad, and the roads were passable. The closer I got to the church, the muddier it became. Finally, a half hour from the church, I came over a little rise and saw the bridge over a small creek in front of me blocked by a truck that had broken down on the bridge. It was the only way to the church, and if I walked, I wouldn't get there until two in the afternoon. I knew God had told me to come, so I just prayed. Then I walked down to the bridge and asked the men there if they could push the truck onto the road so I could pass. Then I saw that the front tire was off the bridge. The men asked me where I was going and I told them I was going to preach at a local church. They talked for a bit and then turned to me and said, "Let us call our friends." After a few minutes, there were twenty of them. They went up to my car and picked it up! Carefully they carried it across the creek. I realized if I had brought the Land Rover, I never would have made it. The service was wonderful and more than a hundred people were saved."

Question

Am I timid about sharing my faith? Am I ashamed of the testimony of our Lord? Am I willing to share in suffering with Christ?

Pray

Father, I desire Your Spirit of power, love, and discipline. I want to fulfill my holy calling for which You saved me. Please give me Your Spirit of boldness and holiness.

DAY 9

Obedient Love

"If you love Me, you will keep My commandments."

John 14:15

Why Obey?

With apologies to my sister—this is her story, but it is such a good story that I must use it here—I share the following:

My sister's family was camping at an African game park. The camp was on a riverbank with a large sandbar stretching out into the river. The baboons at this park were terrible! They would watch to see which child was unable to defend himself then swoop down and take food out of the hands of the smallest and dash off. Sometimes they would steal a whole bag of chips or loaf of bread. So we kept slingshots. Les, my sister's son, was made responsible for "patrolling" one morning. He was nine years old. He loved that job. That morning, he was down on the sandbar looking up at the trees for baboons. The brown river water blended with the tan and burnt sienna of the rich soil being eroded by the river. Across the stream, brush covered the river bank. Hornbills flew overhead. The river flowed softly, peacefully across the plain.

As my sister came out of her tent, she looked down at Les patrolling the riverbank for baboons. Not eight feet behind him, a large crocodile was easing out of the water, mouth gaping open! Looking up at the trees, he did not see the crocodile. My sister, afraid to scare her son so much that he would freeze but also needing him to move quickly, called to him, "Les, come here right now!" Thankfully, without questioning, without hesitation, without pausing to complain, without rationalization or protest, he obeyed. He heard something in her voice that told him to be obedient. His obedience saved his life. The crocodile paused and then disappeared beneath the brown murky waters.

Little do we know sometimes that our obedience to God doesn't just show our love for Him. It also protects us from the roving lion, seeking whom he may devour. Obedience is for our sake not His.

Question

Are you willing to obey without question or hesitation? He may call you to adventure. He might stretch you beyond your comfort zone. Are you ready? Is your answer, "Here am I, send me"?

Pray

Change my heart to make it soft, quiet, and obedient. Keep me from having a stiff neck. Teach me obedience, and from my obedience, know that I love You.

DAY 10

Pardoned

Who is a God like You, who pardons iniquity and passes over the rebellious act of the remnant of His possession? He does not retain His anger forever, because He delights in unchanging love."

Micah 7:18

A Serious Mistake

My job at dusk was to run to the generator house and start the generator. The great machine was the only source of our electricity and we ran it each evening for several hours. My friends helped me with this task. In the dark of the settling dusk, we attached the crank to the engine, turned on the fuel line, and cranked away. At first the engine coughed, trying to start. Diesel fumes filled the little room. Then, with a roar, the engine would ignite. We pulled off the crank and chased each other to the house. At least that's how it went until one fateful night. We performed the usual routine and ran to the house. I remember noticing the lights seemed extra bright as we ran up. We played on the porch not noticing the unusual brightness. It lasted for about ten minutes, and then the lights suddenly died. The distant sound of the generator fell silent. Dad took a flashlight and went to check. He discovered that I had failed to check the governor for the engine speed. Somehow it was set way too high, and the engine had burned out the generator. It was a terrible blow. It meant no electricity for several months while we waited for parts ordered from Europe.

When I found out I was the cause of the disaster, I expected the worst punishment. I remember praying that God would help my parents to forgive me. They were so mad at me. The only statement I received was that they would talk about it. I knew that meant they were deciding my punishment or which boarding school to which they would ban me. Instead, they had mercy on me. Dad told me they decided to forgive me. He didn't feel he had taught me how to check the governor well enough to punish me for my grievous error. I was completely forgiven, though left in the dark for three months.

Question

Aren't you thankful that God does not retain His anger forever? Each of us has our own sin story, but God delights in unchanging love. When was the last time you thanked God for His unchanging love?

Pray

Who is a God like You, who forgives me for my sin and has compassion on my soul? Thank You that You turn Your anger from me and forgive me. Thank You for Your unchanging love.

DAY 11

Lesson From A Tree

He has told you, O man, what is good; and what does the LORD require of you but to do justice, to love kindness, and to walk humbly with your God?

Micah 6:8

Stealing Peaches

We were on stateside assignment for a year. I was five and in kindergarten. Our neighbor had a peach tree, and as fall approached, the peaches grew heavy on the tree. I asked our neighbor if I might have some of those delicious peaches. She was very gentle in her answer, telling me that I was welcome to some when they were ripe, but I must wait a month. This seemed a little strange to me because in Africa, we ate green fruit all the time. If you waited till it was ripe, someone else would eat it before you. Well, this five-year-old was not willing to wait a month. So, the next day, I went over to her house and ate a ton of green peaches. I sprinkled them with sugar. They were delicious! However, that night, my belly was not happy. I groaned and moaned at bedtime. Eventually, I confessed to my parents the cause of my unhappiness. This resulted in some discomfort to my backside as well as my belly and the next day an apology to the peach tree owner. From physical pain, I learned about humility and justice. I've never looked at a peach tree the same way since. I have even learned to like ripe peaches.

We struggle sometimes trying to know what God's will is for our lives. We want to know which college major to choose, or whether we should move to a new job. Though these are important issues to God, they are not the most important to His heart. When we ask Him for direction and guidance, we should first remember Micah 6:8. He has told us what He desires. Justice, kindness, goodness, and humility are what God calls us to.

Question

Are you kind? Are you just? Are you good? If you are all those, are you also humble?

Pray

Teach me to be kind to the hateful, just to the weak, good to the downtrodden, and humble before the praises of men.

DAY 12

Love Demonstrated

God demonstrates His own love toward us, in that while we were yet sinners, Christ died for us. Much more then, having now been justified by His blood, we shall be saved from the wrath of God through Him. For if while we were enemies, we were reconciled to God through the death of His Son, much more, having been reconciled, we shall be saved by His life.

Romans 5:8-10

A Child, a Death

The telegram arrived after the event had already happened. I didn't know what Mother had just read, but I knew it was bad. She sat on the couch in our living room. Through the window behind her lay the Kyela Valley. It was a spectacular view, but her back was turned to it and tears flowed down her face. It wasn't until later that I learned the telegram told of her mother's death and the date of the funeral. The date had passed by the time the telegram arrived.

The next day, twenty-one pastors came to our home. Some had woken early in the morning and walked for hours to be there. They ministered to my parents, consoling them. In the only way they knew, speaking in Swahili, they spoke of heaven and God's love to their missionary. They sang hymns, naturally harmonizing with each other. At the end, they took up an offering. It totaled two dollars. They gave this to my parents to help. My parents couldn't refuse this gift of love, even though they knew that some of these men had given a month's worth of wages. Mom did not see her mother's grave until two years later when we were on stateside assignment.

You know you are seeing God's love when those you have mentored share God with you in your time of need. After we are reconciled to God, we are no longer enemies of God, but friends. We share His love with one another and carry each other's burdens.

Question

Do you demonstrate God's love to others? Do you give what you have?

Pray

Father, create in me a love. Let Your love in me be a demonstrated love, not a hidden love. Saved by Your life, help me to lay my life down as a holy sacrifice, acceptable to You.

DAY 13

House of Grace

For a day in Your courts is better than a thousand outside. I would rather stand at the threshold of the house of my God than dwell in the tents of wickedness. For the LORD God is a sun and shield; the LORD gives grace and glory; no good thing does He withhold from those who walk uprightly. O LORD of hosts, how blessed is the man who trusts in You!

Psalm 84:10-12

Dwelling in Grace

The home I grew up in was originally a barn. My parents converted it into a home over several years. I remember when we got gas lamps so we could see at night. We had screens on the windows; we never needed glass because it was never cold. We had a tin roof covered with thatch to keep the house cool. Instead of walls, my bedroom had slats that blocked line of sight but allowed air through. It was a great day when we put indoor plumbing into the house. We used a fifty-five-gallon drum as a hot water tank. The heat came from a fire under the drum which we started every night. At night we read books or played games. When I was older, we got a television and a VCR. We watched M★A★S★H repeatedly. Dad taught me how to play chess. I learned to play hearts and canasta and forty-two. It was a great place to grow up; a great place to live.

There is a home that is not made of bricks or straw or cement. It is not a barn or a mansion. It is a spiritual home in God. David describes his longing to dwell in the house of God. One day in God's home is better than a thousand days without Him. Whatever each of us remembers about the home we grew up in, good or bad, God's home of grace is where we belong. His home of grace is the best home, the best place to dwell. In His arms we find protection, love, purpose, peace, growth, and grace. No good thing does He withhold from His children.

Question

Do I dwell daily in His home of grace? Do I yearn for Him as David yearned for the Lord?

Pray

Father, I want to dwell in Your grace and glory. I ask for Your blessing. I trust in You, only You.

DAY 14

Trials

Therefore, having been justified by faith, we have peace with God through our Lord Jesus Christ, through whom also we have obtained our introduction by faith into this grace in which we stand; and we exult in hope of the glory of God. And not only this, but we also exult in our tribulations, knowing that tribulation brings about perseverance; and perseverance, proven character; and proven character, hope; and hope does not disappoint, because the love of God has been poured out within our hearts through the Holy Spirit who was given to us.

Romans 5:1-5

Seventeen

When I was about five years old, my parents and my brother Richard and I drove from Kigoma, Tanzania, to Dodoma. Ordinarily it's a five-hour drive. We started out around noon on the excellently maintained, dusty gravel road. After an hour or so, we had a flat tire. No problem. We changed out for the spare. Then we had another flat tire. No problem. A handy patch kit is an essential part of a Tanzanian missionary's car kit. So we took out the inner tube, found the hole, and patched it up. Then, using our handy foot pump, we filled the tire with air and off we went. Until a half hour later, when we had another flat tire, same tire. We repeated this ritual for a total of sixteen times. The seventeenth flat tire found us an hour from our destination at 1:00 a.m. The moon shown brightly. We jacked up the Land Rover, and I watched Dad and my brother repeat the process of removing the tire again. We were in a tropical forest. As they removed the tire, we heard some elephants begin trumpeting nearby. As Richard and Dad tried to find the seventeenth hole to patch, the trumpeting grew louder and angrier and closer. Trees were being knocked down. In alarm, Dad told me to get in the car. As fast as they could, they put the rim back on the vehicle and when it was attached, they lowered the jack and threw the offending tire on the roof rack. We zoomed off, bumping on the bare rim. I just glimpsed elephants through the back window as we drove off.

Seventeen flat tires. That was not a trip to repeat. My brother learned how to fix a flat tire really fast, and I had fun watching. Dad, from then on, had the record for the most number of flat tires on one trip by any missionary. Perseverance and trials create character.

Question

Do trials shake you? Does God bring tribulation to you for a reason? Are you thankful for God teaching you character and hope?

Pray

Father, when You bring tribulation, give me perseverance. From that perseverance, give me proven character. In my trials, I ask for Your hope. Pour out Your love within my heart.

DAY 15

Quiet Love

"The LORD your God is in your midst, a victorious warrior. He will exult over you with joy, He will be quiet in His love, He will rejoice over you with shouts of joy."

Zephaniah 3:17

A Child Loved

Paulo, our cook, in some ways raised me. For a time he lived in a small house on our property with his family. He was the one who fed me snacks when I wandered through the kitchen in search of goodies. When I was five, I was required to take a nap every day after lunch. I discovered that I could escape through my window right after I was put to bed, sneak across the yard to Paulo's house, and spend an hour there. He would serve Safe, his son, and me a bowl of rice with gravy. We would laugh and play and talk. Then I would sneak back to my room (all this in my underwear), tuck myself under the covers, and wait for a few minutes. My parents would come in and "wake me up."

Paulo was always there for me, always in quiet ways helping me. He didn't have to—he was a cook—but his kindness was always there for me. His was a quiet love. Paulo had three fingers missing from his right hand, blown off in the Second World War. He was numb in his hands from the same explosion. He could pull a pan from the oven without using an oven mitt. Watching him everyday I witnessed quiet love living out a life of kindness.

Our Lord God is a victorious warrior, but He is quiet in His love. He rejoices over us when we turn to Him. His touch is gentle.

Question

Is the God you know a gentle God? Does He rejoice with shouts of joy when you turn to Him?

Pray

Teach me Your love, Father. Teach me Your quiet love. Help me to obey You, that I might give you reason to rejoice over me with shouts of joy! I pray that my Father will be in the midst of my life every moment of every day.

DAY 16

The Knowledge of Grace

The God of our Lord Jesus Christ, the Father of glory, may give to you a spirit of wisdom and of revelation in the knowledge of Him.

Ephesians 1:17

Great Grace

An old story among the Nyakyusa (the tribe among which my parents were missionaries) was that one day white people would come and tell them of the true God. Until that time, they worshiped on hilltops leaving small sacrifices to many gods.

We traveled to different villages on Sunday for church. Once we arrived, the pastor would ring the church bell. This consisted of beating a wheel rim suspended from the nearest tree with a metal rod or spike. The clanging of the bell announced church would begin soon. We would sit under a mango tree. The women would soon arrive, sitting on the right. Teenagers and choirs sat in the middle, and the old men sat on the left. The women wore *kangas,* which were brightly colored large rectangular cloths they wrapped around and around themselves. If they had a baby, they would use a second kanga to suspend the child on their back. When the child was fussy, they would swing it to the front and nurse it during the service. When a consensus had arrived, the choir would start off with a series of songs. They stood and swayed in unison while they sang. Natural African harmonies mixed with the rhythm of a small drum would fill the Sunday morning air. The preacher, often Dad, would then share the story of the goodness of God's grace. It was usually a simple sermon. At the invitation, usually someone would come forward to ask for salvation. Their hearts were so open to the story of grace. Many times we were asked why hadn't someone come before to tell them of this story. It was such an important story, they knew it should be shared with everyone.

Question

Have I shared the story of God's grace? As I walk in the mercies of His grace, do I desire for others to have the same fortune?

Pray

Father, thank You for rescuing me. Help me to share this great grace with others who do not know of Your mercy. Thank You for the person who led me to You.

DAY 17

Comforted by Grace

Now may our Lord Jesus Christ Himself and God our Father, who has loved us and given us eternal comfort and good hope by grace, comfort and strengthen your hearts in every good work and word.

2Thessalonians 2:16-17

A Mother's Touch

It had been an extremely long day. We were finally returning home from a long journey, and my parents had driven extra hours to reach our home. We left at five in the morning and by evening, we were still far from home. I was starving as the sun set. Unlike the average American trip, there were no fast food restaurants or other places to eat along the way. It was ten at night by the time we reached our home. I was nearly crying with hunger. My kind mother built a fire in the woodstove. From our pantry, she pulled out some beef stroganoff she had canned months earlier. She put rice on the stove when the fire was hot enough, and by eleven we were sitting down to a piping hot beef stroganoff and rice dinner. It was one of the best meals I can remember. It was not just good because of my hunger, but also because I knew how much work it was for my mother to get that meal to the table. I felt loved by her hands, by her presence, by her hard work on behalf of a little boy who was hungry late at night.

I sometimes think how much more our Father loves us, how much more He desires to comfort us than our mothers. How He longs to soften the blow of pain and sorrow and hunger. We sometimes flippantly make fun of the shortest verse in the Bible, "Jesus wept." We miss the point that Jesus wept because He wanted to comfort His people. He wanted to gather His people like a mother hen gathers her chicks under her wings.

Our God, our Father, wants to give us comfort. He will strengthen our hearts. He fills us with hope buoyed by grace, lifting us from our downcast thoughts to look to Him. His love, comfort, hope, grace, and strength are eternal. They do not last just for one meal; they last beyond our need.

Question

Am I willing to accept God's comfort? Am I willing to submit to His will, to follow Him?

Pray

Father, for our frail hearts we ask Your strength. For our sick, we ask Your healing. For our sorrow, we ask Your comfort. For our failures, we plead Your forgiveness.

DAY 18

Love for a Son

Now it came about after these things, that God tested Abraham, and said to him, "Abraham!" And he said, "Here I am." [God] said, "Take now your son, your only son, whom you love, Isaac, and go to the land of Moriah, and offer him there as a burnt offering on one of the mountains of which I will tell you."

Genesis 22:1-2

First Love

The first time the word *love* appears in the Bible is in this twenty-second chapter of Genesis. Does that seem odd to you? It seems like the Bible should start out with the word love. Yet here it is, twenty-two chapters into His story. Isaac was Abraham's evidence that God fulfilled His promises. You see, God told Abraham that his children would be as many as the stars someday. Sarah, Abraham's wife, laughed when she heard about this promise to her husband. She laughed because she was too old to bear a child. Yet bear him she did, and his name was Isaac. Abraham loved Isaac with all his heart.

So God tested Abraham's love. Did Abraham love God or the son God gave him more? It was a simple test, but one of overwhelming challenge. Do you think that Abraham said to himself at least once, "Maybe I heard God wrong. I am sure God would never ask me to sacrifice my son."

A Jealous God

God describes Himself as a jealous God. He wants to be our first love. He wants to be before our families, before our spouses, before ourselves. He knows that He made us to love Him first. When we get sidetracked into loving the created (even our children) above the Creator, we lose our first love. We lose the very reason He made us.

Question

What loves do you have that are above your love of Him? Finding the answer is simple. Where do you spend the most time? What do you dream about? It may be a new car or it may be an only child. All of us have a tendency to lose our way, falling in love with created things instead of the Creator. Can you, like Abraham, place that thing that you love, maybe your only thing, on the altar and let it die?

Pray

I want to love God above all else. I want to love Him more than my time, more than my independence, more than my family, more than myself. God, help me to sacrifice to You all that holds me from You. It is only through Your strength that I can love You first.

DAY 19

Seeking

So I gave my attention to the Lord God to seek Him by prayer and supplications, with fasting, sackcloth, and ashes. I prayed to the LORD my God and confessed and said, "Alas, O Lord, the great and awesome God, who keeps His covenant and lovingkindness for those who love Him and keep His commandments, we have sinned."

Daniel 9:3-5

Dreamer

A voice called out, "Hodi, Hodi," which is the Swahili way of knocking. The missionary did not recognize the man at the door. "I have come to speak with you about God." The missionary welcomed him into his home. The man explained he was from a county to the south of where the missionary lived. In a dream, God told him to seek out the missionary. The two talked but the missionary explained that he was too busy with his current work and he could not come to tell the man and his village about Jesus. The man had walked for two days to visit the missionary.

Several weeks later, the missionary heard, "Hodi, Hodi," from his doorway. As he went to the door he recognized the man who had visited him before from the south. He welcomed him in and they spoke again. The man explained that God had come to him in a dream again, and he was compelled to come to the missionary again to ask. He begged the missionary to come to his village. This time the missionary could not refuse. From that beginning came a great work of God in Tanzania.

Question

Would you be willing to leave your family and walk for two days to find someone to teach you the truth of God? Would you seek him a second time after being turned down the first time?

Pray

Give me the heart of Daniel. Give me the desire to seek You Father, to bow before You with prayer, supplication, and fasting. I confess to You, God, that I have sinned. I have not sought You with all my heart. It is from You that I need forgiveness. From You, I plead for a seeker's heart.

DAY 20

Washed Grace

He saved us, not on the basis of deeds which we have done in righteousness, but according to His mercy, by the washing of regeneration and renewing by the Holy Spirit, whom He poured out upon us richly through Jesus Christ our Savior, that being justified by His grace we would be made heirs according to the hope of eternal life.

Titus 3:5-7

Wash Day

Like many families, we had wash day every week. For us it was on Thursday. All the clothes of the family were collected and dumped into appropriate piles on our screened porch. Then we filled the gasoline tank on our washing machine and fired up the unbearably loud engine. For the next five hours, the noise deafened all involved. After each load, we ran the clothes through the wringers attached to the washing machine. Care was taken with the wringers because they could wring fingers just as well as clothes. The clothes were left to dry overnight. We hung the clothes on the screened porch because if we hung them outside, flies would lay eggs on the clothes and we would all get fly larvae growing in our skin. On Friday, the clothes were taken down and lovingly folded. Dad's shirts and pants were ironed with a charcoal iron. If the hot coals spilled on the clothes, it would burn holes in them.

Sometimes when the Spirit is renewing my mind and soul, I think it is a lot like wash day. God's word washes away my dirtiness and greed and apathy. Then the Spirit puts me through the wringer, squeezing out my ungodliness, leaving behind only obedience and self-control and the other gifts of the Spirit. As I dry, I must be careful what I put back into my mind or fly larvae will crawl into my mind and grow new seeds of greed and lust and pride.

Thankfully, the Spirit is poured out upon us so richly that if we allow Him, we are continually renewed into His likeness. As we are changed, we grow less desiring of self and more desiring of God's heart and His love. Wash day must happen every day, or I start to drift unknowingly toward my own desires.

Question

Am I washing myself daily with God's word? Am I choosing to listen to Him instead of the distractions of the world? Am I willing to accept God's wringer, to allow myself to be squeezed into the shape God desires?

Pray

Father, give me a longing to be with You daily. Pour out into my life the rich mercy of Your Spirit, washing me and renewing me into who You designed me to be. Give me the desires of Your heart.

DAY 21

Every Day

The grace of the Lord Jesus Christ, and the love of God, and the fellowship of the Holy Spirit, be with you all.

2 Corinthians 13:14

Grace

The definition of grace is unmerited favor. Grace is the gift of love God gives us that we don't deserve. God showed us His grace by sending the Lord Jesus Christ to die to pay our debt for wrongs we have committed. But I am not so interested in the theological definition of grace. I am interested in my personal gift of grace.

When I was five years old, I received my personal gift of grace. I remember telling Dad that I felt bad for doing wrong (you may recall my stealing of the peaches), and I wanted God to forgive me. Dad led me to ask Jesus into my heart and helped me ask for forgiveness. Little did I realize it then, but the debt I owed was much greater than a five-year-old could perform. I realize now that God sees my whole life, every wrong thought and action I will do in my short seventy or eighty years. When Jesus died on the cross, He offered to me forgiveness for my whole life of wrongs. All my wrongs are nailed to that cross. Even the wrongs I will do ten years from now. Everything of my whole life, paid for before I'd even done them. Wow! That is grace! He is a good God to forgive me of so much.

Did you notice in the verse above, the last part, "the fellowship of the Holy Spirit"? I love that part. You see God didn't just pay for our debt. Jesus didn't die just for forgiveness. No, He died because He likes us and He wants to talk to us every day. He wants to spend time with us (fellowship). He wants to help us grow spiritually. He wants us to thrive in our relationship with Him. How do we forgive ourselves and others the way He has forgiven us? By the Holy Spirit. How do we understand the grace with which God loves us? By the Holy Spirit. While I was yet scornful of God, He chose me, loved me, died for all my life's wrongs, and now His Spirit lives in me, transforming me daily with His grace.

Question

Do I realize what grace is to me? Am I thankful for His love? Do I like to spend time with God, this God who gave His life to spend time with me?

Pray

Father, I ask for the grace of Jesus, the love of God, and the friendship of Your Spirit. I ask that, every day, You will overwhelm me with Your grace.

DAY 22

Faithful Love

"Then it shall come about, because you listen to these judgments and keep and do them, that the LORD your God will keep with you His covenant and His lovingkindness which He swore to your forefathers. He will love you and bless you and multiply you; He will also bless the fruit of your womb and the fruit of your ground, your grain and your new wine and your oil, the increase of your herd and the young of your flock, in the land which He swore to your forefathers to give you."

Deuteronomy 7:12-13

A Heart Broken, Mended

I remember a time when my father received a letter from my older brother. The letter described how my brother had rejected Christ and rejected all that my father was doing as a missionary. It was a crushing blow. I was only five years old at the time, and we were living in Tanzania. My father decided to fast and pray. Every day for a week, he would come to the table and sit with us and not eat. At first I was just surprised, then concerned that Dad was not eating. Then, seven days later, Dad came to breakfast and ate with us. He told us that God had answered his prayers; we need no longer worry. Little did we know God had answered the prayer thirty-five years earlier.

My dad's best man at his wedding was not a Christian. So, Dad prayed for him. He prayed for his salvation for thirty years before his friend accepted Christ.

Five years later—the summer after my dad received that letter from my older brother—Dad's friend led my brother to Christ. The next summer, my brother came to Tanzania and taught me to memorize Scripture. I still have my first book of Scripture memory verses, preserved in nearly illegible six-year-old scrawl.

Question

Are we faithful in our prayers? Are we ready to be faithful for thirty years? The Lord your God will keep you with His covenant and His lovingkindness.

Pray

Father, I am weak in my love for You. I need Your strength to walk after You. I need Your Spirit so that I might be holy before You. I need Your sustaining power that I might remain faithful in my walk with You. I love You. Help me to keep Your judgments and do them.

DAY 23

Love from Him

"This is My commandment, that you love one another, just as I have loved you. Greater love has no one than this, that one lay down his life for his friends."

John 15:12-13

How to Love and Forgive

If you have never read *The Hiding Place* by Corrie Ten Boom, you have missed something in life. Corrie, along with her sister Betsie, was incarcerated in a German concentration camp for helping Jews escape persecution from the Nazis during WWII. She suffered hunger, fleas, beatings, and the death of her sister at the concentration camp. After the war, Corrie traveled to more than sixty countries telling of Jesus' love and forgiveness. One day in Munich at the end of a service where she had spoken, a young man came up to speak to her. In her words:

> [He was] the former S.S. man who had stood guard at the shower room door ... at Ravensbruck. He was the first of our actual jailers that I had seen since that time. And suddenly it was all there—the room of mocking men, the heaps of clothing, Betsie's pain-blanched face.

> He came up to me as the church was emptying, beaming and bowing. "How grateful I am for your message, Fraulein". he said. "To think that, as you say, He has washed my sins away!"...

> I tried to smile, I struggled to raise my hand. I could not. I felt nothing, not the slightest spark of warmth or charity. I breathed a silent prayer. *Jesus, I cannot forgive him. Give your forgiveness.*

> As I took his hand, the most incredible thing happened. From my shoulder along my arm and through my hand, a current seemed to pass from me to him, while into my heart sprang a love for this stranger that almost overwhelmed me.

> And so I discovered that it is not on our forgiveness any more than on our goodness that the world's healing hinges, but on His. When He tells us to love our enemies, He gives, along with the command, the love itself.

— From *The Hiding Place* by Corrie Ten Boom

Question

Am I ready to obey His call to love one another? Am I ready to forgive deep pain caused by others? Am I ready to love the undeserving, the unlovable, the unforgivable? Am I ready to lay down my life for Him who laid His down for me?

Pray

Teach me of this great love, Jesus. Teach me to love others as You have loved me. Help me to have the greater love; the love You command, the love You give.

DAY 24

Prayer of Grace

For this reason I too, having heard of the faith in the Lord Jesus which exists among you and your love for all the saints, do not cease giving thanks for you, while making mention of you in my prayers.

Ephesians 1:15-16

Ceaseless Grace

Early morning started when the roosters crowed. The cool morning air wafted into my room through the window which was only covered in screen to keep out the mosquitoes. No glass was needed as it never was cold enough. Birds sang outside my window. This still of the darkness was interrupted by the faint touch of light coming from above the mountains to our east. Even that early I knew that our cook, Paulo, was lighting the fire in the woodstove and he would be boiling water for tea soon. I rose to cross the hall to brush my teeth, and out of the corner of my eye, I saw Dad kneeling next to his bed, praying. It was a place I often saw him. He was placing his day in God's hands.

A few minutes later, Dad went out and started the farm work. I heard the tractor rumble to life. Its diesel gurgle was a friendly sound. I dressed and went to my desk to prepare for a day of school. Outside, cocoa plants rustled in the morning breezes. They were small trees, and the pods on their trunks contained the cocoa seeds. Mom passed by me, headed to the kitchen to prepare breakfast. The light around us grew until the first rays of the sun warmed the tin roof. Morning was upon us. Breakfast consisted of fresh fruit salad and poached eggs with toast from the woodstove. The bread was homemade with a thick crust. The butter was churned by hand from the milk from our cows. It was the kind of breakfast you remember for its goodness. After breakfast, we read a short devotional and prayed for the missionaries who had their birthdays that day.

Question

Do I give God's grace to others through my prayers? Am I obedient in my prayers, praying without ceasing? No matter the morning, do I pray, putting my day into His hands?

Pray

Father, I place today into Your hands. I pray Your grace will be poured out on my friends and on those around me today. I pray for my children and my parents, that You will guide them and be with them and fill them with Your love. I pray that they will walk in You today.

DAY 25

The Name of Grace

I pray that the eyes of your heart may be enlightened, so that you will know what is the hope of His calling, what are the riches of the glory of His inheritance in the saints, and what is the surpassing greatness of His power toward us who believe. These are in accordance with the working of the strength of His might which He brought about in Christ, when He raised Him from the dead and seated Him at His right hand in the heavenly places, far above all rule and authority and power and dominion, and every name that is named, not only in this age, but also in the one to come.

Ephesians 1:18-21

Holy Grace

There was a time when I was young that the work of the gospel in southern Tanzania was at a critical stage. The churches were growing and the missionaries were busy and new work was beginning in many places. A new district commissioner was appointed to our area. A district was like a county in the United States. The commissioner had power far beyond any county commissioner in America, however. He could govern in any way he wished, and he could establish any new law he desired. He could even imprison anyone who refused to follow orders. I am sure many a county commissioner in the United States wishes he had this much power. This new commissioner was a Muslim. One day as he was out driving around his new territory, he noticed a sign for a new Baptist church. As he continued driving, he saw many church signs. Angry at the number of churches, he declared a law that no church could erect a sign announcing its presence. He threatened to kick the missionaries out of the district.

This became a matter of intense prayer and fasting. My parents wrote to America to ask for prayer. We were afraid that the work would be stopped or even persecuted by this new threat. Everyone began to pray for God to intervene and change the heart of this Muslim.

One day the man dropped dead. No one was sure why or what had caused his death. The result was immediate. The man's replacement was friendly to the church work. The church signposts were put back up and life continued on as before. No one had prayed for the man's death, but the results were unmistakable. The sovereign Christ who has all authority worked through the prayers of His people and made certain that His church would continue to grow.

Question

Do I fear the God I serve? Do I acknowledge His lordship in my life? Am I obedient to Him?

Pray

Father, I praise You for Your Holiness. I praise You for Your majesty. I praise You, Christ Jesus, for dying to pay my sin debt. I praise Your name, the name above all names in this age and the age to come. I thank You for Your gift of grace. I praise You, Holy Spirit, for teaching me Your word and turning my heart to You. I praise You for every good thing in my life which is a gift of grace from You.

DAY 26

Grace Abundant

I thank Christ Jesus our Lord, who has strengthened me, because He considered me faithful, putting me into service, even though I was formerly a blasphemer and a persecutor and a violent aggressor. Yet I was shown mercy because I acted ignorantly in unbelief; and the grace of our Lord was more than abundant, with the faith and love which are found in Christ Jesus.

1 Timothy 1:12-14

How Much Grace Do We Need?

I stared into the three-gallon tin. In the darkened coolness of the hut, the water appeared like crystal. "Why do you have this water sitting here?" I asked my friend Safe.

"Mother walks each morning to the river and brings water to the house. Then she lets the water sit so the dirt will fall to the bottom of the tin. If we need more water than that, then we have to walk to the river."

Every day of every year, someone in that family had to walk to the river and bring water back to the home. I thought of my home. I just turned on the faucet, and water came out. If I wanted to drink water, I used filtered water. Even at my home, though, I had to keep drinking the water when I was thirsty. I thought about the woman at the well who talked to Jesus. He offered her living water. Once you drink living water you never thirst again, He told her.

That is how much grace we need. We need grace that once given, covers all our violence, all our greed, all our pride, all our gluttony, all our sin for our whole life. We need grace to change us, to transform us so that we become kind, honorable, compassionate, gentle, and humble with self-control. Christ Jesus our Lord's grace is abundant. It overflows into our lives, spilling onto others around us. His grace is not just sufficient for every sin we will ever commit, it is abundant beyond measure. In Him are found mercy, grace, faith, and love. We never have to walk to the river again, thirsty and dry, tired or weak. He is our living grace.

Question

Am I walking as one transformed by grace or as one trapped by sin? If I am forgiven by Christ Jesus the Lord, have I forgiven myself? Do others see grace flowing from Christ through me, or do they see me as thirsty, always seeking a new well?

Pray

Father, thank You for Your abundant grace. Thank You for transforming me into Your child. Thank You for Your living, flowing water of grace.

DAY 27

Strong Grace

You therefore, my son, be strong in the grace that is in Christ Jesus.

2 Timothy 2:1

Different Strengths

A Volkswagen Beetle is many things, but "strong, powerful vehicle" is not among its attributes. I found myself, at six years old, crammed into the little space intended for a suitcase behind the backseat. We were touring a game park, and as usual we were looking for lions. Lions are difficult animals to find because there aren't very many of them, and they hide in the shade during the day. They hunt and kill at night—the daytime is for rest and relaxation. Our guide suggested we enter a large clump of trees on an otherwise flat, grassy plain. I am sure he thought the lions might be hiding beneath the trees. Somewhat of a surprise to all of us, especially Dad (who was driving) and the guide (who was in the passenger seat) as we rounded a corner, we came upon a very angry, enormous bull elephant. It stood towering above us, trumpeting. Its large tusks seemed especially threatening. Our Beetle suddenly seemed like a flimsy tinfoil can compared to that enormous elephant blocking our way. I, of course, could only see part of the elephant from behind the backseat. I felt the car reverse and, looking back, I saw tree branches whipping by as we retreated. We only partially followed the path, but I don't think Dad cared how bumpy the retreat was.

Its odd though, when I think of strength—strength in grace—I don't think of that elephant. I think of my parents. I think about how they pray every day for my family. How they have dealt with so many setbacks in their lives and never given up. How little they complain when there are so many times things have gone against them. They taught about the strength of His grace to others, themselves examples of staying the course no matter the storms. I think their grace is strong because every day they spend time with the author of grace. Nothing can stop you if you are strong in the grace that is in Christ Jesus; although you may retreat to another path if you meet an angry bull elephant!

Question

Are you weak? He has told us that in our weakness, He is made strong. Are you frail? He heals us. Are you discouraged? Be of good cheer for in our limitations, He is glorified. Are you afraid? Only turn to Him daily for the boldness of Christ.

Pray

Father, give me the desire to be with You daily. Let my strength come from Your grace instead of my accomplishments. When the world tells me to be self-sufficient, let me be grace-sufficient.

DAY 28

Perfect Love

But in all these things we overwhelmingly conquer through Him who loved us. For I am convinced that neither death, nor life, nor angels, nor principalities, nor things present, nor things to come, nor powers, nor height, nor depth, nor any other created thing, shall be able to separate us from the love of God, which is in Christ Jesus our Lord.

Romans 8:37-39

Overwhelming Force

We were at a mission meeting in Lemuru, Kenya. It was a large complex, and our little cottage had a roaring fire to combat the fifty-degree temperature outside. My brother Richard pulled out the Risk game, and over a week we played every night after the conference meetings. Near the end of the week, we were still playing the same game. Risk is a game of territory and world domination (a great game for boys). Due to several lucky breaks and my brothers attacking each other, I was able to gradually take over the game. At last only one country was left, Brazil. I had hundreds of armies, and my older brother had one army left. I possessed every country in the world but his. You can imagine the delight of the youngest brother beating the whole family. I amassed all my armies on the border and attacked with overwhelming force. Game over. I did some little dance and was immediately warned to clean up the board and put it all away. Younger brothers are not supposed to dance victory dances. I am certain neither of my brothers remember my epic victory.

From this little illustration comes a picture of our walk with God. Through Him, we overwhelmingly conquer. How? We conquer through His love. We often feel that God doesn't like us because we are shallow and our self takes over and we struggle with sin. Paul tells us that nothing can separate us from His love. I often hear people try to put exceptions into this statement, but there are no exceptions. Nothing can separate us from the love of God. What about my own failure and rejection of God? Notice that Paul says no "created thing." Are you created? Then you cannot separate yourself from God's love. Nothing can separate you from His love.

Question

What is my response to His love, this love of overwhelming power, overwhelming grace, overwhelming compassion, overwhelming mercy? Do I love in return? Am I passionate about this great God?

Pray

Be in me the love You deserve. Be in me the faith I lack. Be in me who You are. Be in me the love of God.

DAY 29

Fragrance

Therefore be imitators of God, as beloved children; and walk in love, just as Christ also loved you and gave Himself up for us, an offering and a sacrifice to God as a fragrant aroma.

Ephesians 5:1-2

Walk in Love

Going through the trash seemed like a perfect plan. I was six and the trash can at the end of our long driveway contained an endless supply of treasures, not the least of which was my mom's old, broken lipstick. You can just see what happened next. Well, let's just say I had red lips and cheeks and hands and arms and about anything I could lipstick. All was well until my mother discovered my new decor. I was brought to Dad and a spanking was recommended. (Mom generally recommended a belt, and usually her guidelines were followed.) On this particular day, a different, far more terrible, punishment was instituted.

Charlie Johnson was a young man who worked with missionaries on our station. He was a young man from the United States who had worked with my parents for two years, and he was my hero. I wanted to walk and talk and look like Charlie Johnson. So, Dad, wise as he was, pronounced my punishment. "If you have any lipstick on you at dinner, I am going to tell Charlie Johnson."

You cannot imagine the horror this scenario created. I was devastated. I rushed to the bathroom and spent the next two hours scrubbing my skin like it was a dirty bathtub. Periodically, I would look in the mirror and return to scrubbing. I tried soap and vinegar and dirt and toothpaste and baking soda. I think the red on my skin was from irritation more than a remnant of the lipstick.

Dinner went well. Dad choose to ignore the faint extra redness of my face and lips and arms. At prayers, I prayed that Charlie Johnson would never find out about my lipstick disaster.

I often wish I had as much passion to imitate God as I had when I was that six-year-old boy who wanted to be like Charlie Johnson.

Question

Do I walk in love, the same love that Christ had when He was sacrificed for me? Am I a fragrant aroma to God?

Pray

Father, give me the strength to love Your instruction, follow Your ways, and dwell in Your understanding. Teach me to meditate on Your word. Let my life be a fragrant aroma to You.

DAY 30

Precious Gift

But we believe that we are saved through the grace of the Lord Jesus, in the same way as they also are.

Acts 15:11

School

My desk was perfect for first grade. It had a white Formica top with little silver stars. It had a little rubber-rimmed bumper around it. I could stick my pencil into the rubber and leave a mark without breaking the lead. There were many marks. Above the desk, my window looked out on tall trees and blue sky. Each morning after breakfast, Mom would sit with me and teach me. I spent most of my time looking out the window and jamming my pencil into the rubber rim. Mom and I learned A to Z. She must have been bored with the material but there was no other teacher; she was it. So, we learned together.

Now, many years later, I think about the gift my mother gave me. I learned to read and write at her instruction, literally at her knees. The foundation she built into me allowed me to attend college, go to medical school, and even write this devotional. It was a gift. It was not a gift I appreciated much at the time. I was much more interested in playing and looking outside. How could I understand this gift? It is a gift that has lasted my whole life. I will only know the sum of the gift as I reach the end of my life and look back, only then understanding what was given to a little six-year-old boy.

Grace given by the Lord Jesus is the same. When we accept His gift, we have no idea of its cost or power or the change it will bring. Even at the end of life, we will not know its true whole. Only when we are with Him on the other side, will we realize how precious is His gift of grace.

Question

Am I grateful for His precious gift of grace? Am I walking with Him obediently, or am I seeking my own way, taking His grace for granted?

Pray

Father, thank You for Your grace. Thank You that every day, every minute, every heartbeat, Your grace changes my heart, changes my mind, and changes my spirit. You sustain me; You raise me up; You forgive me. You—only You—give the grace I need. I bow before You.

DAY 31

His Purpose

And we know that God causes all things to work together for good to those who love God, to those who are called according to His purpose.

Romans 8:28

Little Lessons

The little Volkswagen Beetle hummed along the dirt road. My parents were in front. My brothers took up the backseat, and I was sitting in the little storage compartment behind it. The family was excited because we were going on vacation to the coast of Kenya in Mombasa. A week at a beach resort was very exciting. My parents, trying to find a shortcut, had learned that there was a road which cut through the Tsavo game park. We were warned to be out of the park by dark because there was little traffic, and if we had car trouble it would be dangerous because of the wild animals. Naturally, if you know our family, darkness arrived long before we had reached the park exit. Before darkness arrived, the drive was fun. We saw wildebeest, impala, and zebra. After darkness fell, the adults talked, enjoying the time to be together. Then, the lights went out.

Everyone climbed out of the Beetle. Mom held the flashlight while Dad and my brothers tried to figure out why the lights had stopped working. I just watched till I got tired. Finally, Dad decided to pray. We all bowed our heads out there in the middle of the African plain and asked God to turn on the lights, literally. After we prayed, I got back in the car and laid down on the backseat. Suddenly, I heard a cheer from the front of the car. I jumped out to see what had everyone so excited. The headlights were on. They closed the hood and the lights went out. I stayed out for a bit as they fussed and worked, then went to lie down again. As I laid down, I heard another cheer. As I exited, the lights went out. It suddenly dawned on everyone that when I laid down, the lights came on. They pulled up the back bench and sure enough, a wire was loose. When I had laid on it, the lights came on.

I learned at a young age to depend on God. To some, these were just circumstances; to me, God works for good because I am called according to His purpose.

Question

Do I trust Him to work all things together for good for me? Am I walking after His purpose?

Pray

Help me to trust Your purpose for me. Give me Your perspective so that I will trust in Your love. As You call me for Your purpose, give the strength and desire to follow.

DAY 32

Flowing Grace

Then when he had arrived and witnessed the grace of God, he rejoiced and began to encourage them all with resolute heart to remain true to the Lord; for he was a good man, and full of the Holy Spirit and of faith. And considerable numbers were brought to the Lord.

Acts 11:23-24

Seven-Year-Old Eyes

Our home had been invaded by eleven American pastors and several members of their churches. They had come to help with a revival. I don't remember their names except the leader, Bobby Welch. He was a dynamic pastor, with energy and typical American humor. The teams went out to several churches and schools, preaching three times each day. People came to hear them because they were white. American visitors were rare to our district in Kyela, Tanzania. Each evening Mother tallied the number of people who had accepted Christ at each service for each team. I remember we had set a hopeful goal of a thousand decisions.

One night, one of our pastors recounted the story of his day. He was asked to help a sick person in the village. He explained he was not a doctor, but he would pray for the person. As he entered the darkness of the hut, he noticed a man lying on the floor. The person did not respond when he prayed. The pastor wondered how soon the man would die—he was obviously gravely ill and seemed to be in a coma.

He walked with his translator to the next preaching point. Not long after he began preaching, a large group of people walked up and joined the group under the mango tree. He restarted his sermon. This pattern repeated itself three times until there was a large crowd of people seated on the ground in front of him. A fourth time he began, and then his translator stopped him. "Look, there is the man you prayed for!" Coming into the clearing was a older man who was dressed in the same clothes as the one he had prayed for just an hour before. The man spoke, "I am the one you prayed for. God has healed me. We have come to listen to your message."

At the end of the revival, Mother tallied up the numbers and just before we prayed together one last time, she announced that over eleven thousand people had accepted Christ during the revival. I saw this with my own seven-year-old eyes. With my eyes, I saw grace flowing from Him, through His children to the lost. "Considerable numbers were brought to the Lord."

Question

Am I remaining true to the Lord? Am I walking with Him, encouraging all around me to receive the grace of the Lord?

Pray

Father, let the grace You have given me flow to others, touching all who know me and all who need me.

DAY 33

Cling to Love

You shall follow the LORD your God and fear Him; and you shall keep His commandments, listen to His voice, serve Him, and cling to Him.

Deuteronomy 13:4

Cling to Him

The word *cling* is a picture word which describes little chicks rushing to hide under their mother's wings when danger threatens. Another image to describe this word is a child clutching his mother's leg, desperate for her protection. In Psalm 119:31, the psalmist says, "I cling to Your testimonies."

My seventh Christmas is my most memorable. My mother, infected with an amebic abscess in her liver, lay in a hospital room in Nairobi, Kenya. On Christmas morning, I opened a big yellow Tonka dump truck my parents had bought two years earlier, while we were on stateside assignment. I went outside on the grounds of the hospital and played with my new Tonka truck. Dad and I spent a few hours with Mom. She was very weak. Then Dad and I went back to our missionary hostel. I learned later that, as my mom clung to life in that hospital room, she prayed to God that He would spare her life so that she could stay and raise me, her last child. Forty years later she is still with us, still clinging to God.

The Lord is our protector. He is a strong fortress, a strong tower, a shield. When life's storms threaten, He is there. I have had my share of troubles. Every time, I seem to have trouble remembering that my Father is the King of Kings and Lord of Lords. I tremble like a leaf when storms blow, somehow forgetting His hand is upon me. Yet as I look back upon my life, I realize that as I cling to God, He protects me. His protection has kept me safe. In His strong tower, I am safe. I am safest in His arms.

Question

Are you clinging to God? Is He your protector, your defender?

Pray

When I am afraid, protect me. When my body fails me, give me strength. When my eyes are blind, give me sight. When those I love are sick, heal them. Give me the strength to cling to You. Protect me in Your strong tower.

Edson L. Knapp

DAY 34

Where His Glory Dwells

I will go about Your altar, O LORD, that I may proclaim with the voice of thanksgiving and declare all Your wonders. O LORD, I love the habitation of Your house and the place where Your glory dwells.

Psalm 26:6–8

A Place of Love

Our kitchen when I was growing up was an amazing place. It didn't look that great, but it was a place a kid wanted to be whenever possible. The wall paper was beyond faded. The smoke from the woodstove stained the warped ceiling tiles. But out of that oven came delicious breads and desserts. In the summer we would help squeeze lemon juice. My mother and our cook, Paulo, would mix the lemon juice with enough sugar to make a thick syrup. Then all year long, we drank fresh lemonade from those bottles of syrup and lemon juice. I remember making butter with Paulo. I was amazed to see that yellow goo appear out of that white cream. Whenever I was hungry, there was something in the kitchen to eat, something good and yummy. When I was injured or hurt, I could go to the kitchen to see Mom for a Band-Aid and a hug. It was a place of love.

Each child of God has the glory of God dwelling within him or her. It is the place where His glory dwells. Just as David loved going to the temple, so our hearts are to be a place where others long to come. We are the habitation of God, and it is through us that others often see Him.

Question

Are you a place of love? Do others see His glory dwelling within you? Is there something in your kitchen (your heart) that keeps others from meeting God when they come to you? Are you a hug or a shrug? Are you too busy for their interruption?

Pray

Father, I want my heart to be clean before You. I ask You to cleanse me from unfaithfulness, from sin, from selfishness and busyness and the pursuit of created things. Give me a pure heart that others might find Your glory dwelling within me. Then, I will declare Your wonders and voice my thanksgiving for a place of love, Your love within me.

DAY 35

Fullness of Grace

He put all things in subjection under His feet, and gave Him as head over all things to the church, which is His body, the fullness of Him who fills all in all.

Ephesians 1:22-23

Cold Climb

As a seven year-old, I was finally allowed to join my older brother Richard on some of his many mountain climbs. He was nine years older than me and spent much of his time off from boarding school climbing the mountains in southern Tanzania. The tallest mountain in our area was Mount Rungwe. It was 9,710 feet tall. My brother, Dad, and I set off to climb it. We started our climb from the back of the volcanic mountain in the fog—which should have been a warning about the ensuing climb. The first portion of the climb was through a dense pine forest. Brown nettles covered the ground like a woven mat. Eerily quiet, we heard only our packs shifting and our own breathing. As we emerged above the forest, it began to drizzle. Though our packs were waterproof, we were not. The temperature dropped, the wind picked up, and before long I was freezing. After two hours, we reached the crater floor. Because of the cold, we decided to set up camp and change into dry clothes. After a cold supper, I snuggled down between my brother and Dad. Water condensing on the inside of our small tent dripped onto my face during the night. The next morning, cold and tired, we climbed to the crater rim. It remained foggy, though thankfully the rain had abated. After an hour, we reached the rim. In another hour we reached the peak. Just as we came to the pinnacle of the mountain, the fog lifted. Before us the entire southern highlands of Tanzania was laid out like a green carpet. It was stunning! Tired but elated, we simply sat and watched the beautiful world beneath us. Eventually, we rose and retraced our steps down the mountain, our hearts full of happiness.

That view in some small way is like the fullness of Christ which fills us with grace. We struggle with the valleys in our lives. We struggle with relationships, finances, and stress. But from time to time, God pulls back the curtain, and we behold the fullness of Christ. It takes our breath away. It reminds us of whom we serve and of His holiness. That is when we realize that all our pettiness and worries are just vapors evaporating in the radiance of His glory.

Edson L. Knapp

Question

Am I lost in the fog or living in the knowledge of the glory of His grace? Does my faith remain strong in the foggy world of life?

Pray

Father, fill me with the radiance of Your glory. When all around me is vague and shadowy and stressful, remind me that You are the King of Kings. Your name be praised and may Your light extinguish the darkness around me.

DAY 36

God's Own

For the grace of God has appeared, bringing salvation to all men, instructing us to deny ungodliness and worldly desires and to live sensibly, righteously and godly in the present age, looking for the blessed hope and the appearing of the glory of our great God and Savior, Christ Jesus, who gave Himself for us to redeem us from every lawless deed, and purify for Himself a people for His own possession, zealous for good deeds.

Titus 2:11-14

Purified by Grace

On Sundays when we went out to visit a church, Mom always took a large thermos of boiled and filtered water. That was our water for the day. I quickly discovered the penalty if I strayed from that container. Usually by Sunday night, my stomach would start churning and Monday was spent sitting or kneeling before the white throne. After a few rounds with that experience, I found the water in the thermos to be very important.

There was one place that the water was pure and clean. When we hiked up into the mountains, the water in the streams was pure and cold and delicious and, most importantly, clean. The water washed down through four thousand feet of waterfalls and rocks and moss and trees and crystal pools. In the valley, hot with humidity shimmering across the rice fields, that water was unbelievably wonderful. It was one of the best parts about hiking. We would climb and get hot and uncomfortable, only to find ourselves at the foot of a waterfall. We drank and skipped stones and some of us put our feet in the water.

God gives us streams and pools and waterfalls of grace. His grace transforms us, freeing us to live sensibly and righteously. His grace redeems us from contamination and purifies us. By His grace we become His children.

Question

Am I willing to let the rocks and falls purify me? Am I willing to be refined as gold in the fires of life that God sends my way? Am I willing to become grace-purified?

Pray

Father, forgive me for my dirtiness. Purify me, filling me with Your grace, Your hope, Your mercy, Your faith, and Your love. Let all people know that I am God's own, that I belong to You and to no other.

DAY 37

Grace Received, Grace Given

Be kind to one another, tender-hearted, forgiving each other, just as God in Christ also has forgiven you.

Ephesians 4:32

Skipping Stones

There is something wonderful about a still pond of water and flat, smooth stones along the bank. I remember when I first learned to skip stones. The Mwalisi River near our house had several ponds, and the banks were filled with flat worn stones washed out of the mountains. They were different colors, black and tan and white with streaks. The water flowed along, chirping and burbling until it entered a flat patch and formed a pond. That was where a group of friends could spend a whole summer afternoon skipping stones across the water. The goal was the most number of bounces while reaching the other side. The water was clear. Reeds surrounded the far bank. The hot afternoon sun reflected off the water. Rings of little waves scattered out from the bounces of our stones. We threw a mountain of stones into that pond over the years.

The grace God gives us is, in some ways, like skipping stones. You find the perfect flat stone and you are so excited. You throw it really hard with just the right spin. Then the rock turns wrong, and it plops into the water on the first bounce and disappears. Your heart just sinks, it's so disappointing. I think God is disappointed a little like that when He gives us grace, just the right way, grace made just for us. Then, instead of reflecting the grace to others around us, we let the grace die inside of us. We remain greedy or unforgiving or unkind. The grace sinks inside our hearts and disappears. It makes God sad when that happens. If we reflect His grace to others, it pleases Him. It gives Him joy to see His grace reaching others, bringing light and joy into lives as we pass His gift of grace to those we can touch. The rings of grace scatter out from our lives, touching others He places in our lives.

Question

Am I tender-hearted? Am I forgiving? Am I kind? Am I angry or bitter? Do I grieve my Father?

Pray

Father, thank You for Your grace. Thank You for Your tender heart, Your kindness, and Your forgiveness of my failures. Help me to reflect Your love to others. Help me to share the grace You designed for me to give to others in my life. You are my grace received; let me be Your grace given.

DAY 38

Planned Grace

In Him also we have obtained an inheritance, having been predestined according to His purpose who works all things after the counsel of His will, to the end that we who were the first to hope in Christ would be to the praise of His glory.

Ephesians 1:10-12

Days of Fear

Fever … dreaded fever. Malaria is a killer. Each year more than one million African children die from its deadly embrace. I was fourteen, and my body was racked with chills. It was evening and though my body was blazing hot, I pulled the covers over me, trying to ease the shaking chills. My head ached and pounded with each heartbeat. Dad gave me Chloroquine. I heard my parents murmuring about their fears that the malaria was becoming resistant to the reliable drug we used to treat the infection. Then the fever broke. I could sense their relief. The night passed almost peacefully. In the morning I awoke, drenched in sweat again. I was shaking. My headache worsened. I felt heat coming off my body as I shook from waves of chills. My mother took my temperature and pronounced the dreaded treatment. She started a cold shower and forced me into the freezing water. Far from any medical help and with limited drugs, she knew this was the quickest way to bring down my now dangerously high fever. I shivered and shook as the cold water drenched me. I could only stand it for a few moments. After I dried off and dressed, she took my temperature. Shaking her head, she told Dad we must leave to get medical help. The trip took almost three hours. By the time we arrived at the hospital in the afternoon. I was delirious. Malaria, a parasite, grows in the red blood cells. In fever-producing waves, it breaks open the cells and then enters a new cycle infecting new cells. The victim dies of lack of oxygen because there are not enough red blood cells left to carry oxygen to the body.

At the hospital, the doctor gave me IV fluids and a new drug called Fansidar. The malaria in our region had not yet developed resistance to that drug. Within twelve hours, my fever abated. Why did I survive? It was the purpose of Him who works all things after the counsel of His will.

Question

Do I trust Him with my life? Many asked my parents if they were afraid of taking their children to such a remote place to live as missionaries. Their reply, "We are safest following His will, relying on His mercy."

Pray

Father, help me to see Your hand of grace upon my life. Help me to know that what comes tomorrow is by Your will and Yours alone. Give me the faith to trust today, no matter the challenge, be it cancer or depression or come what may. Let me declare to You, Lord: "I trust in You."

DAY 39

His Mercy

But God, being rich in mercy, because of His great love with which He loved us, even when we were dead in our transgressions, made us alive together with Christ (by grace you have been saved).

Ephesians 2:4-5

Blue Sky

My high school was more than eight hundred miles by air from southern Tanzania where I lived. The school, International School of Moshi, was built at the foothills of Kilimanjaro. At the end of each three-month term, I would return via a small missionary plane to my home in Mbeya where my parents would meet me. It was always such a joyous time of reunion.

On one particular day, the pilot helped me load my suitcase into the single-engine Cessna, and we took off. After forty-five minutes, the pilot frowned and removed his headphones, his head cocked to one side. He turned to me and said, "The engine is missing. I am not allowed to carry passengers when there is a problem with the engine. I will drop you off." He replaced his headphones.

Five minutes later, he landed on a dirt strip barely twice as wide as the plane. He placed my suitcase on the dirt track. "I'll try to find someone on the radio to pick you up." With that he closed the door, turned the plane on a dime, and disappeared into blue sky. I sat on my suitcase taking in my surroundings. It was complete wilderness. Brush surrounded the strip. Nothing stirred. It was hot. A stray fly, surprised at my presence, delighted in tormenting me. I waited. Nothing. I waited. Three hours later, a plane buzzed out of the blue sky and landed. When it reached me, the pilot opened his door and called out, "Are you Edson?" I thought the question strange. How many boys were sitting on their suitcases in northern Tanzania on that day? Just over two hours later, I saw my parents waiting for me as we landed in Mbeya. The reunion was especially joyous that day!

Have you ever felt like everything was lost, like everything was falling in on you? Have you ever felt completely alone? That really, completely alone feeling churning at the bottom of your heart? I think that is when God loves to come to us in His rich mercy. Those are the times when we can deeply know His great love. That is when we discover we are not alone; we are with our Father, the King of Kings.

Edson L. Knapp

Question

Do I trust God when everything is falling in on me? Or do I get grumpy and frustrated? Do I kick the dog or go to my knees? Do I rely on His mercy or my own strength?

Pray

Father, give me faith that Your mercy, grace, and love will be there when I fall, or when I am alone, or when my friends turn against me. Turn my heart to You.

DAY 40

Perfected Grace

Therefore humble yourselves under the mighty hand of God, that He may exalt you at the proper time, casting all your anxiety on Him, because He cares for you. Be of sober spirit, be on the alert. Your adversary, the devil, prowls around like a roaring lion, seeking someone to devour. But resist him, firm in your faith, knowing that the same experiences of suffering are being accomplished by your brethren who are in the world. And after you have suffered for a little while, the God of all grace, who called you to His eternal glory in Christ, will Himself perfect, confirm, strengthen and establish you. To Him be dominion forever and ever. Amen.

1 Peter 5:6–11

On Alert!

We walked up to the reception area, a large hut joined by an open porch with the kitchen and dining huts. The huts were thatched with stone walls. Beyond the reception hut, each room was its own separate canvas tent attached to a brick and mortar bathroom. Beyond the area of the camp, the grassy, dry, African plain stretched out as far as we could see. It was hot but not unbearably so. As we approached the reception area, two men were scrubbing the stone floor. They were cleaning what appeared to be blood. I asked the smiling African behind the counter how the blood got spilled there at the reception area. He replied, "Last night a lion killed a gazelle here in front of the reception. They are cleaning up the mess." As he saw us look around uneasily, he laughed. "Do not be on alert now, during the day; the only danger is at night." As we were staying the night, the words did not seem so comforting. That evening, an armed guard escorted us to and from our tents for dinner. We were on alert!

Though threatened by our adversary, the devil, we are children of the God of all grace who called us to Him. Though a gun may protect from an African lion, it is only God's strength which can establish us in safety. His mighty hand provides our protection. His tender care comforts us. Because He was one of us, He understands our fears and anxieties. He regards our suffering with sympathy, knowing our weaknesses. Though the lion roams, seeking our destruction, we are under the protection of the God of all grace.

Question

Am I courageous, believing in the protection of God? Do I behave boldly as a child of the King? Am I humble, casting my cares on His mercy and grace?

Pray

Father, from my weakness, show Your strength and power. Give me humility that I may be strong in You. Calm my fear of the lions in my life, strengthen and establish me as Your child.

DAY 41

Every Blessing

Blessed be the God and Father of our Lord Jesus Christ, who has blessed us with every spiritual blessing in the heavenly places in Christ.

Ephesians 1:3

Sufficient Grace

In the eighties, my sister was a missionary in Ethiopia. (This is her story, which I am thankfully retelling here.) Her husband was heavily involved in famine relief and was gone for days at a time into the countryside. When he was home, he was so busy she hardly saw him. If you remember the images on TV, there were thousands of children dying of starvation. The country, one of the poorest in the world, had no food. My sister found herself raising three children by herself with a compound to run. She grew starved for her husband and for male attention. In her own words, "My Father does care for my needs ... all of them. I needed male affirmation. I knew that. So one day, I remember pulling up the blinds as I reluctantly started my day. *ALLLLLLLL my needs, huh God?* Well, I am going to trust You to meet this one. I need male affirmation, and I trust You according to your riches in glory."

A communist revolution had swept the country several years earlier. To help prop up the communist government, Cuba had sent a large military force to Ethiopia. Little known to my sister, a large contingent had returned to Addis. The road to the market passed along a long, straight corridor. The bumpy potholes ensured that the drive was a slow one. As my sister turned onto this road, she realized it was lined by a huge number of Cuban soldiers, waiting in their trucks. As she saw them, they saw her. As she recounts, "I had to go to town alone. Usually I traveled with a group of others because gas was rationed during the war. When they saw me, some of them climbed on top of the trucks. They leaned way out. They jumped up and down. They cheered. They waved. They whistled. They threw kisses. I was a one-woman parade for a group of very lonely soldiers whose women were on the other side of the world. I started crying as I drove because it was such an amazing answer of my heavenly Father to my trust that He knew and would take care of my needs. How much He does love us. He will move a whole bunch of people across an entire country to take care of our needs." And that is one of her life stories about how God takes care of us no matter where we are or what we are going through. She always tells the story with a smile at the memory. We are blessed, and our Father knows our needs. We often fail to ask.

Question

Where do I turn for my needs? Am I dependent on God, the only true answer to my needs?

Pray

Father, I ask You for my daily bread. I ask you to meet my needs. I ask You to help me to be thankful for what You have given and not to grumble about the things I want. I ask You to use me to care for the needs of others.

DAY 42

Prayer of Grace

Grace to you and peace from God our Father and the Lord Jesus Christ.

Ephesians 1:2

He Sees His Children

I was lonely. I was overwhelmed and very forlorn. I had just entered boarding school and suddenly found myself eight hundred miles from home in the ninth grade. The school was advanced, and I was failing every class. I had not developed any quick friendships, and boarding school was not as fun as I had expected. One Saturday, a young missionary showed up at the school and asked for me. I had never met her before and have never talked to her since that day. She introduced herself and we sat out in the yard of my dorm and talked. She explained that during her prayer time, she had felt God tell her to come and find me and talk to me. She didn't know why, but she wanted me to know that God knew of me and what I was going through. Over the next two hours, I told her of my struggles with school and of my loneliness. I told her how I had contracted chickenpox and how I was struggling. We sat in a little, worn, wooden gazebo with Kilimanjaro in view. She gave me some counsel, prayed with me, and left. It was such a touch of love from God. I felt Him telling me that He was with me and saw my trials. He had compassion and grace upon me.

Many times in my life, His hand has touched me—often through someone else who is praying for me. I know His heart is with me. His grace is upon me, no matter the trials through which I pass. When Paul wrote to the Ephesians, his first prayer for them was that the grace and peace of God would be upon them.

Question

Do I know without doubt that His grace is with me? Do I trust Him through every worry and fear? Am I ready to share His grace with others in need? Am I willing to be interrupted by His plan for me to share His grace with another?

Pray

Father, I ask today for Your grace to me. I ask for Your grace to my church and to my friends and to those for whom I pray. I ask today for forgiveness for my worry and anxiety. Instead, fill me with the peace of Your grace. Father, I rest in Your hand, Your hand of grace.

DAY 43

Joined In Grace

I am confident of this very thing, that He who began a good work in you will perfect it until the day of Christ Jesus. For it is only right for me to feel this way about you all, because I have you in my heart, since both in my imprisonment and in the defense and confirmation of the gospel, you all are partakers of grace with me.

Philippians 1:6-7

Water Partaker

My chemistry teacher unfolded a plastic container. We watched as he filled it with three gallons of water from the small stream. We were climbing Kilimanjaro, and a small sign marked the stream as the last point of available water. Above this level, there were no more streams. The stream flowed through tundra which froze each night. Moss and grass grew along the stream. Giant groundsels of senecio grew across the landscape. They were ten to fifteen feet high with what looked like cabbage plants at the top. Dead leaves covered the upper trunk, protecting it from the cold.

I lifted the container of water onto my already heavy pack and started carrying it up the trail. I could not possibly have carried the water the whole day. We took turns about every half hour. As we walked, the landscape changed, becoming rock fields strewn along the valleys and ridges. The terrain became more dramatic with cliffs next to our path falling away hundreds of feet below us. That evening we camped in a tin hut bolted to a ridge with five hundred foot cliffs falling away on each side. After a supper of soup from the water we had carried, we tried to sleep as winds buffeted the tin hut. In the morning, we finished the water, pouring it out into our canteens. We knew that by evening we had to be down to water. We were all partakers of it.

Just as all of us need water, all of us need living grace for eternal life. Like Paul, we partake of the grace of Christ Jesus. It is through His grace that He perfects us until the day when we see Him face to face. We need living grace more than we need water. Thankfully, grace is free, requiring no work or payment. There is no point of last grace.

Question

Are you a grace partaker? Is living grace more important than water to you? Are you walking in His grace today, at this moment?

Pray

Father, thank You for the grace You have given me. Thank You for paying the price of my grace, a cost I could not pay. For Your living grace, I give thanks today.

51

DAY 44

Redeeming Grace

In Him, you also, after listening to the message of truth, the gospel of your salvation—having also believed, you were sealed in Him with the Holy Spirit of promise, who is given as a pledge of our inheritance, with a view to the redemption of God's own possession, to the praise of His glory.

Ephesians 1:13-14

Drenched and Buried

Dad had the very special task of baptizing new believers. In the days of the revivals, as I have mentioned in previous devotions, there were many who, having accepted Christ, needed to be baptized. On Sundays, after a long church service (Dad often preached through the whole Bible), we would have a baptism. Even though I was hungry and thirsty by this time, I enjoyed these second services. After another sermon and introduction of the new members, the whole congregation would walk, singing together, to the nearest river. Some of the places we went were a little threatening. There were the dangers of snakes and parasites and even the occasional crocodile. On one particular day, we ended up at a murky brown pond surrounded by elephant grass. The church members stood on the banks and sang as a line of baptismal candidates formed. At the end of each verse in the song, we would pause and wait as the person in the brown water was buried into the muddy water and then raised up. The younger ones smiled as they rose. The older, more dignified new members tried to ensure their clothes were properly placed. Water dripped from them onto the dusty soil as they walked up out of the river. Each one was welcomed into his or her new family. Many times, fifty or sixty people were baptized.

As Paul said in Romans 6:3-4, "Do you not know that all of us who have been baptized into Christ Jesus have been baptized into His death? Therefore we have been buried with Him through baptism into death, so that as Christ was raised from the dead through the glory of the Father, so we too might walk in newness of life." All who have accepted Christ are sealed in the Holy Spirit. We are buried in baptism and raised to a new life, life in Him.

Question

How often do I forget that I belong to Christ Jesus? Do I behave as a child of the King of Kings, filled with His Spirit? Have I forgotten His redeeming grace, the sealing into His Holy Spirit, the promise of His glory?

Pray

Father, remind me today of my need for You. Remind me that I am Yours, paid for by the greatest sacrifice. Remind me of Your grace for me, in me, and moving through me.

DAY 45

Elohim—God, Mighty Creator

In the beginning God created the heavens and the earth.

Genesis 1:1

Creator

Over the next few days, we are going to review the Hebrew names of God. I love His names and what they tell us about Him. The names help us learn to love Him and teach us that God is love.

Elohim, which means mighty creator, is the first name of God we find in Scripture. When God made us in His image, He included his wonderful attribute of creativity. I love all the amazing things people do out of creativity. Of course, some have more talent than others. For example, my brothers and sister have great musical ability, and I have none. When I was taking guitar lessons in eighth grade, my oldest brother told me to quit because I had no sense of rhythm and I wasn't very good at the melody either.

In the beginning God created. ... Do you see who made us? Do you hear the words of the One who knit us together? He created. Love created. Love is creative. On a simple level, think about the first time a boy tries to write a love note. If it's creative and original, it's a good note. If it's a copy, it's boring. He must not really love the girl. Look at God's creativeness. Look at all the creatures in the world. Look at the variety on earth. Look at the universe—it is filled with endless creativity. Love is creative. God desires creativity from us. I think He probably loves women a little more than men, since He gave them the gift of creating life within themselves.

When God created the world, He pronounced it to be good, very good. Why did God love what He made? He made it from love. He spoke love into physical reality. It was good. We, His children, are made *from* love *to* love. We are made to be creative.

Question

Do you worship a creative God? Do you give Him your creativeness? Do you honor Him with adventure?

Pray

Father, give me Your creative love. Create in me anew the desire to create for You, the desire to make the gift to show You I love You.

DAY 46

Adonai

I said to the LORD, "You are my Lord; I have no good besides You."

Psalm 16:2

Adonai—Lord

"I have no good besides You."

A favorite childhood memory for me is of my family singing hymns together. Usually, we would be driving across Tanzania, and we would have talked about everything in each others' lives. Someone, often Dad, would decide it was time to sing. The Land Rover would hum along, and we would join in, voices in harmony. I use the term "we" loosely, since I've never sung a harmony in my life—unless, of course, it was by mistake.

One of my favorite hymns was "Come Thou Fount of Every Blessing." I know the words seem old, and I never quite understood "mine Ebenezer" (found in 1 Samuel 7:12, if you want to look it up). The lyrics are wonderful and every time I read them, I pray them to God. "Jesus sought me when a stranger, wandering from the fold of God; He, to rescue me from danger, interposed His precious blood." And I love, "O to grace how great a debtor, daily I'm constrained to be! Let Thy goodness, like a fetter, bind my wandering heart to Thee. Prone to wander, Lord, I feel it, prone to leave the God I love; here's my heart, O take and seal it, seal it for Thy courts above."

My heart is prone to wander. I pray so often for God to take my heart and change it so it won't desire to walk in disobedience.

Question

Whom do I serve? Do I obey my Lord, my Adonai? How often I sit at His feet and renew my vows to follow Him, yet as I walk away from His side, I return to the same old habits.

Pray

Adonai, my Adonai, bind my wandering heart to Your side. Take my heart and seal it with Your Spirit. Upon Your grace I fling myself, knowing without Your grace I would be lost, a wandering stranger far from goodness, far from the God I love.

DAY 47

Yahweh

God said to Moses, "I Am Who I Am"; and He said, "Thus you shall say to the sons of Israel, 'I Am has sent me to you.' "

Exodus 3:14

Yahweh—Lord.

In Moses' time, the people of Israel had grown in number to become a small nation, but they were slaves in Egypt. They were suffering terrible persecution, including the slaughter of their male children. Into this world of pain, the God of Abraham, Isaac, and Jacob revealed a new name to Moses. This name, "I Am Who I Am," is the name by which God wanted to be remembered always: "Thus you shall say to the sons of Israel, 'The Lord, the God of your fathers, the God of Abraham, the God of Isaac, and the God of Jacob, has sent me to you.' This is My name forever, and this is My memorial-name to all generations. Go and gather the elders of Israel together and say to them, The Lord, the God of your fathers, the God of Abraham, Isaac and Jacob, has appeared to me, saying, 'I am indeed concerned about you and what has been done to you in Egypt' " (Exodus 3:15-16).

Repeatedly, the Lord reminds us that He is concerned about us, that He loves us. This is not some theoretical "spiritual" concern, but it is a love that is intimate and full of compassion and caring. This is greater than the love a mother has for her newborn child. His love is greater than the love of a father when his son hugs him after winning his first Little League game. This love of our Father is protection and adventure all wrapped into one joyous life with our Maker.

This God, Yahweh, created time, created the universe, and created me. He planned my life, my every moment before I was born. He is in my yesterday, my now, and my tomorrow.

Question

Do I trust Him to forgive me for my yesterdays? Do I follow Him in my today? Do I trust Him for my tomorrows?

Pray

Father, Yahweh, I ask You to restore to me my yesterdays, guide me today, and give me peace for my tomorrows.

DAY 48

El-Shaddai

Now when Abram was ninety-nine years old, the LORD appeared to Abram and said to him, "I am God Almighty; walk before Me, and be blameless."

Genesis 17:1

El-Shaddai—God Almighty

El-Shaddai, God Almighty, is the all-sufficient, all-powerful God who can accomplish His purposes among us. When Abram was ninety-nine years old, God Almighty appeared to him and announced a covenant between them. God Almighty changed Abram's name to Abraham (from father to father of a multitude). Sarai's name was changed to Sarah (from mother of one family to mother of a nation). Abraham's response to the announcement that God would give them a child was to laugh out loud. What man of one hundred years and wife of ninety years can bear a child? Only a couple who have a covenant with El-Shaddai.

"Walk before Me, and be blameless." That is the command of El-Shaddai. He commands that we walk before Him. This command requires a relationship with Him. Think about the garden of Eden when God walked with Adam and Eve every day. The second part of the command must be followed in order for the first to be fulfilled. We must be blameless for God to walk with us. Only through Christ can we be blameless. Thus God's command to Abraham can be applied to us as well. We can daily walk free in grace, free from condemnation, because of Christ's sacrifice. It is the command of El-Shaddai.

Question

How do I respond to my Father when He announces His extraordinary plans for me? Do I laugh in disbelief. or do I walk before Him in faith?

Pray

Father, thank You for Your covenant with us through Your Son. Thank You that I am justified by You so that I may walk with You. Help me to walk with You daily. Let my time with You renew me and build my faith. Let me desire purity and blamelessness in You and You alone.

DAY 49

Yahweh Yireh

Abraham called the name of that place The LORD Will Provide, as it is said to
this day, "In the mount of the LORD it will be provided."

Genesis 22:14

Yahweh Yireh—The Lord Will Provide

When Isaac was born, Abraham knew that this son was God's fulfillment of
a promise to him to become a father of nations. Then God asked Abraham
to sacrifice Isaac as a burnt offering. We read in Genesis 22:6-8, the account
of Abraham walking with Isaac to the site of the sacrifice: "Abraham took
the wood of the burnt offering and laid it on Isaac his son, and he took in
his hand the fire and the knife. So the two of them walked on together.
Isaac spoke to Abraham his father and said, 'My father!' And he said, 'Here
I am, my son.' And he said, 'Behold, the fire and the wood, but where is the
lamb for the burnt offering?' Abraham said, 'God will provide for Himself
the lamb for the burnt offering, my son.' So the two of them walked on
together."

I cannot imagine being the parent walking by the side of my son. How could
I be obedient to the request for my son's life as a sacrifice? Which of my
children would I sacrifice? The truth is, God demands that I place Him above
all, even my family.

In whose hand do I place the lives of my children and wife? Is it my strength that
keeps them safe? Is it my work that provides for them? The answer, of course, is
none of those things are in my hand. All these things are very important to me,
but everything is in the hand of God. He is the only one who can provide. When
I choose Him above all, He provides. When I choose obedience, He provides.
When I depend on Him, He provides.

My whole life, He has provided for me. When I was lonely, He touched me.
When I was fearful, He loved away my fear. So many times, the lives of my
children were out of my hand. The only thing I could do was place them in
His hand. He has only been faithful.

Question

Do I trust Him? Do I depend on Him? Do I expect His hand at my side? Do I place Him above my wife, my family, my work, my income, myself?

Pray

Father, thank You for being my provider. Thank You for providing for my righteousness. In the Lord's Prayer, I see Your provision for my food, for my shelter, for my guidance, and for my forgiveness. You are my provision and in You, You alone, I trust.

יְהוָה רִפָא

DAY 50

Yahweh Rophe

And He said, "If you will give earnest heed to the voice of the LORD your God, and do what is right in His sight, and give ear to His commandments, and keep all His statutes, I will put none of the diseases on you which I have put on the Egyptians; for I, the LORD, am your healer."

Exodus 15:26

Yahweh Rophe—The Lord Who Heals

The people of Israel were led out of Egypt to the edge of the Red Sea. God parted the waters and the Israelites walked on dry land. The pursuing Egyptian army was drowned.

After this triumph, Moses led them into the wilderness and they searched for water for three days. They came upon the waters of Marah, but they could not drink because the waters were bitter. They grumbled and complained. Moses cried out to God and He showed Moses a tree to throw into the waters and the waters became sweet. Then in verse 26, God told them His name: The Lord Who Heals.

Wounded, broken, tired—bring yourself to the God Who Heals. Think of the life of the Israelites. Most people died before age forty. Fifteen percent of women died in childbirth. It was the most common cause of death for women. Pneumonia and skin infections resulted in death. There were no emergency rooms, medicines, or doctors. The only healer for them was the Lord Who Heals. The only healer for us is the same living God. He heals my sickness. He heals my heart. He heals my pain. He heals my tiredness. He heals my anxiety. He heals my depression and suffering. He heals my bitterness. Yahweh Rophe, The Lord Who Heals, can change your bitterness into joy.

Question

Am I willing to let go and let Yahweh Rophe touch me? Am I willing to be healed, or do I hang on to my pain, afraid to release part of my identity?

Pray

Father, heal me from my sinful heart, heal my body so that I may do Your will. Heal my will to be obedient to You. Heal my emotions, calm me amidst the storms.

DAY 51

Yahweh Shammah

The name of the city from that day shall be, "The LORD is there."

Ezekiel 48:35

Yahweh Shammah—The Lord Is There

Ezekiel witnessed his nation going into captivity. He prophesied from captivity in Babylon. Ezekiel called God's people to repentance, warning them they were captives because of their rebellion. In the middle of their despair and captivity, foreigners in a strange land, Yahweh shares a message of hope. God will prepare a city for them and the name of that city will be "the LORD is there," and they will dwell there forever with God. When we fear where we are or where we are going, when we don't know the future, when uncertainty makes our steps uncertain, Yahweh is there.

When the Apollo 8 mission was launched on December 21, 1968, it would be the first time humans orbited the moon. It was also the first time live TV broadcasted images of the lunar surface as the crew orbited over the crater-scarred landscape. The mission was piloted by the crew of Frank Borman, James Lovell, and William Anders. As the space capsule orbited around the moon on December 24, the three astronauts took turns reading from the creation story in Genesis. "And God said let there be light . . ." Then they prayed on live TV. They lived through the adventure and risk of leaving earth and reaching the moon. As they circled the moon, they were 238,857 miles from home. While orbiting the moon, they found Yahweh Shammah, The Lord Is There. No matter where we are, God is there before us. Even in space, far from home, He is there. Whether sickness or health, blind or sight, deaf or mute, darkness or light, prison or free, He is there before us, awaiting our arrival.

Question

Am I ready to believe that God is there before me? Will I remember His presence when I am diagnosed with cancer, when my financial world collapses, or when a family member dies? Will I remember Him when life sends rain and storms instead of sunshine?

Pray

Father, thank You for the times of plenty and goodness and family. Thank You also for the times when I must endure suffering. Help me to remember that in my suffering, You are made strong. Grant me the grace to endure tests and trials. Let me give You glory, come sun or rain.

DAY 52

Yahweh Mekadesh

"You shall consecrate yourselves therefore and be holy, for I am the LORD your God. You shall keep My statutes and practice them; I am the LORD who sanctifies you."

Leviticus 20:7-8

Yahweh Mekadesh—The Lord Who Sanctifies You

To sanctify means to make holy, sacred, to cleanse, or redeem. The Lord is He who sanctifies us. He makes us holy. He calls us to purify ourselves by following His word, His law.

What does a sanctified person look like? I ask myself what does my Father want from me? He is much more interested in practical daily life than He is in religious practices or words. He calls me to be fair to others today. I am to be faithful to my wife today. I am to give my children a hug today. I am to be the best doctor I can be today. I need to spend time with Him today.

I love these verses from Leviticus because they teach us who is responsible for our holiness, who redeems us. We are not made holy by our actions. He is the Lord who sanctifies us. The price He paid to sanctify us was the death of Christ on the cross. By the blood He poured out, we are made holy, we are redeemed, and set apart for purity. As a response of love for His redeeming us, we are to keep His law. I am not bound by the law, I am free under grace to choose to do the things that please my Father. I am free to love my Redeemer. I am free from fear, from selfishness, from hate, from greed—and free, instead, to live a sanctified life. Daily I depend on His grace and His word to transform me into His sanctified child.

Question

Am I choosing to love God every day? Am I kind to the weak, gentle with the downtrodden, caring for the sick? Will I gossip today or lift up others with my words? Will I love my Redeemer today, or will I love myself more?

Pray

Father, thank You for setting me apart as Your child. Thank You for loving me and giving me Your word to show me how to live. Give me Your grace today to walk in Your ways. Change my heart's desires to align with Your desires. Help me to love You. Help me to love others that You have put into my life.

DAY 53

Yahweh Tsidkenu

"In His days Judah will be saved, and Israel will dwell securely; and this is His name by which He will be called, 'The LORD our righteousness.' "

Jeremiah 23:6

Yahweh Tsidkenu—The Lord Our Righteousness

Every day after I finished my homeschool lessons with Mom, I would play with my friends on our farm. During the rainy season, we often saw snakes. One day we saw a king cobra. It was about twelve feet long and up in the trees near our house. We tried to shoot it with our slingshots but it got away. The head of the snake as it reared its neck was impressive. Another snake we saw more than once was a spitting cobra. This cobra tracks the eyes of its attacker, aims, and spits venom into the attacker's eyes up to a distance of six feet. The venom does not hurt the skin, but if it hits the eyes, it causes blindness within minutes.

When these snakes would show up on our property, we would get a large clear sheet of plastic and hold it up between us and the snake. We then approached with spears. The cobra, threatened, tried to shoot its venom. Thwarted by the plastic, the poison fell harmlessly on our clear sheet. We could walk up to the snake and kill it with a spear.

I think about that plastic sheet and how it protected and covered us from the poison of the snake. Though it is a limited analogy, in many ways, this mirrors God's righteousness for us. When we cover ourselves with the blood of Jesus, we are protected from the attacks of Satan. They fall harmlessly, deflected by God's protection. Further, our coat of righteousness justifies us before God so that He sees us as Righteousness. By the death of His Son, He became The Lord Our Righteousness. We are shielded from danger, from punishment, and from Satan by the righteousness of The Lord Our Righteousness.

Question

Do I thank God for becoming my righteousness? Have I made Him my Lord? Do I walk after Him?

Pray

Father, thank You for being my righteousness. Thank You for protecting me and forgiving me of my sin. Thank You for covering me with Your blood.

DAY 54

So Great a Grace

But I do not consider my life of any account as dear to myself, so that I may finish my course and the ministry which I received from the Lord Jesus, to testify solemnly of the gospel of the grace of God.

Acts 20:24

Who Is This Jesus?

Have you ever met a slave? It's an odd question. We don't have slavery in this modern society do we? I was a research assistant helping to test a new psychiatric questionnaire. As a part of our testing, we received permission to go to the state mental hospital. It is a beautiful place out in the middle of nowhere with trees and beautiful landscaping. Inside was a place where hope had been abandoned long ago. I remember one patient I interviewed. I was asking from a list of drugs which ones he might have used. This patient was the only person who answered yes to every single drug on the list. He had sniffed glue and smoked cigarette butts left on the ground. He'd tried everything on my long list, including heroin, LSD, oxycontin, crystal meth, mushrooms, and more. When I was done asking, he paused and asked, "What about diesel? Diesel is good to sniff. Gasoline is not as good, it's harder to get high from." He had red hair, a friendly face, and he seemed intelligent enough. Yet he had abandoned every relationship in his pursuit of getting high. He was a slave. He lived in lockdown. He was a slave, living on a slave's plantation.

Paul was also a slave. He was bought with a price. Paul was in custody, on his way to Jerusalem. From there, he would be taken to Rome in chains. He did not consider that imprisonment to be of any importance. His desire was that he might finish the ministry of telling others of the gospel of the grace of God.

It may be that we are all slaves. We are either slaves to our own desires and hungers and darkness or we are slaves to the grace of God.

Question

Whom do I serve? Do I choose to serve myself on most days? Have I belittled the grace of God by placing it on the shelf of my heart while I pursue my career or my plans?

Pray

Father, I ask for the freedom only Your grace can give. I ask to be Your slave, Your bondservant, Your child. Father, teach me to consider Your grace of greater account than my own life.

DAY 55

True Love?

Let love be without hypocrisy. Abhor what is evil; cling to what is good. Be devoted to one another in brotherly love; give preference to one another in honor; not lagging behind in diligence, fervent in spirit, serving the Lord; rejoicing in hope, persevering in tribulation, devoted to prayer, contributing to the needs of the saints, practicing hospitality.

Romans 12:9-13

What Does Love Look Like?

There was nothing extravagant in their home. Carpets were plain and a little threadbare. The furniture was a collection of hand-me-downs. The big-screen TV, donated. Seemingly random people came by to eat lunch or dinner. Sometimes they had questions; other times they just soaked up the love filling that house. Meals were hot and plentiful, if cheap. Something that smelled delicious was always cooking in the kitchen. The table was big, scarred, and wooden. Love was alive at that table.

I loved visiting them. It was my sister's house. They raised five children in that home. That was after being missionaries for fifteen years in Africa. Much of that time was spent in hunger relief. My sister and her family lost all they had, were arrested and imprisoned before they fled the country. Their firstborn child is buried in Africa.

You see, their love was refined, all the chaff burned away, it had persevered in tribulation. That house was filled with prayer. That was why so many people came to visit. The love was genuine, the care true, the advice direct and tested.

When I want to know what love looks like, I think of that house. I think of the price paid. I think of love offered without fear, without reservation.

Question

Do I give preference in honor? Am I fervent in spirit? Am I serving the Lord, rejoicing in hope, persevering in tribulation? Am I devoted to prayer? Do I practice hospitality?

Pray

Father, I want to have Your love in my home. I want my home to be filled with the sweet perfume of prayer and hospitality. I want to serve You with my love.

DAY 56

Know Love, Know God

For God so loved the world, that He gave His only begotten Son, that whoever believes in Him shall not perish, but have eternal life.

John 3:16

We know love by this, that He laid down His life for us; and we ought to lay down our lives for the brethren.

1 John 3:16

Laying Down Your Life

How many lives have you saved? Now that is an odd question, one that you don't hear every day. I am a doctor, and I know if you got a group of doctors together and asked them that question, many of them wouldn't have an answer. Surgeons sometimes save lives, but to actually save a life is rare. Many doctors, especially doctors who treat cancer, will help people live for several years beyond what they might have, but they don't think of themselves as *saving* those people. I remember saving someone from drowning when I was younger. There was a child in Tel Aviv, Israel. He was a toddler who wandered up to the pool and fell in when his parents weren't watching. I jumped in and pulled him up from the bottom of the pool. My daughter Emily fell into our pool, and I had to jump in to save her. That was with all my dress clothes on. I still remember her standing on the bottom of the pool looking up at me with bubbles coming out of her mouth.

When I think about saving someone's life, it seems so temporary. I think about my dad leading me to know Christ. That was an eternal saving. That changed my whole life and my eternity. That changed my life and the lives of my children. That is the kind of lifesaving God calls us into. Because He laid down His life for us, we ought to lay down our lives for others. We can save the fallen—we can change someone's eternity. Through the grace by which we are saved, we share the good news with others. We participate in God's love. We share the good news, the lifesaving, the *eternity-saving* news of His love.

Question

Am I ready to lay down my life in the same way He laid down His life for me?

Pray

Father, thank You for loving me. Thank You for saving me. You changed my life and gave me joy and happiness. You sustain me every day. Sadness is softened; joy is richer, and life is fuller because of Your love. Father, help me to share what You have given me.

DAY 57

Paul's Prayer

For this reason, I bow my knees before the Father, from whom every family in heaven and on earth derives its name, that He would grant you, according to the riches of His glory, to be strengthened with power through His Spirit in the inner man; so that Christ may dwell in your hearts through faith; and that you, being rooted and grounded in love, may be able to comprehend with all the saints what is the breadth and length and height and depth, and to know the love of Christ which surpasses knowledge, that you may be filled up to all the fullness of God.

Now to Him who is able to do exceeding abundantly beyond all that we ask or think, according to the power that works within us, to Him be the glory in the church and in Christ Jesus to all generations forever and ever. Amen.

Ephesians 3:14–21

The Love of Christ

After the Lord's Prayer, this prayer by Paul in Ephesians is my favorite in the Bible. It is so rich, and Paul is even praying for me (see the last sentence). My favorite part is where Paul talks about God's love and his desire for us to understand or comprehend it. How could anyone ever know the depth or height or length of God's love? Especially when that love surpasses knowledge. Is it possible to know all the fullness of God?

I think of my parents who speak about their love for each other. If you ask, they will tell you that when they married they loved each other with more love than they thought possible. Yet as the years went by, they realized *that* love was only a childish love. Over time their love deepened. Troubles came and went, children grew and married, arguments flashed and were forgotten; all the while love grew. It became deeper and wider and higher. Even now they will tell you as their bodies fail them that their love for each other has grown quietly year by year.

Is this not how we learn about God's love for us? We spend time with Him, and over a life of time with Him, we learn to trust Him. We see His compassion, His plans for good, His rescue, His deepest, widest, tallest love for us. We see it over a life of time, and we come to know His love which surpasses knowledge.

Question

Am I pursuing this God who loves me? Am I learning to love Him as He first loved me? Do I give Him thanks? Do I tell of all His wonders? Do I exult in Him? Do I sing praises to His name?

Pray

Father, I pray from my knees that You will teach me and my family and those I know, according to the riches of Your glory, and what is the breadth and length and depth, and to understand what is the love of Christ which surpasses all knowledge. Amen.

DAY 58

Grace Be With You

The grace of the Lord Jesus Christ be with your spirit.

Philippians 4:23

What Is the Secret of God's Peace?

He wrote from a cell in Rome. In his life he was beaten and whipped times without number, stoned and left for dead, shipwrecked three times, and now he was imprisoned. From that prison cell he wrote to his friends a letter that might be titled "a letter of joy." The advice of this man to his friends, "Finally, brethren, whatever is true, whatever is honorable, whatever is right, whatever is pure, whatever is lovely, whatever is of good repute, if there is any excellence and if anything worthy of praise, dwell on these things. The things you have learned and received and heard and seen in me, practice these things, and the God of peace will be with you" (Philippians 4:8-9). Just before this verse, he advises to be anxious for nothing, instead simply ask God your requests.

Paul's list of trials makes my life seem a little tame. I was unemployed once. I did nearly die from malaria. I am always short of money. I will stop listing my problems now, because next to Paul's problems, mine are embarrassingly small. What was his secret? Why didn't he worry like I do? When Paul advises me to practice thinking on godly things, he is teaching from personal experience, personal trials, personal life. The God of peace was with Paul. I pray that the God of peace will be with me and with you. When there isn't enough money till next payday, when a spouse or child is sick, when a storm hits, even when death threatens—may the grace of the Lord Jesus Christ be with our spirit. We need to let our minds dwell on the loveliness and wonder of Christ's love for us. We need to let His peace comfort us.

Question

Do I waste time worrying and fretting? Am I robbed of joy by the trials of life? Am I troubled and pushed and overwhelmed? Am I willing to accept the grace of the Lord Christ?

Pray

Father, I ask for Your Spirit of grace to be with my spirit. I ask for Your peace, Your perspective, Your patience, Your purpose. I ask that no matter the trouble facing me, Your peace will cover my fear, calm my inner storm, and transform my trials to joy.

DAY 59

JESUS

"She will bear a Son; and you shall call His name Jesus, for He will save His people from their sins."

Matthew 1:21

Yahweh Saves

The name *Jesus* is a Greek name. It is taken from the Hebrew name Joshua. It is likely that Mary and Joseph called him by the Hebrew name Joshua. Joshua is a derivative of two words. The first word is taken from the name of God, Yahweh. The second part of the name, "shua," derives from "yaw-shah" which means "having salvation," or "saves." Thus, the name Jesus means that Yahweh saves, or the I Am Saves. It is often translated "the Lord is Salvation." It is by this name that Yahweh completes the salvation of man, which He began when He called Abraham to sacrifice Isaac on the altar. He was the God who provided the ram in place of Isaac. Now He is the God who provides our righteousness, providing Himself as a lamb, slain for us all.

> Surely our griefs He Himself bore, and our sorrows He carried; yet we ourselves esteemed Him stricken, smitten of God, and afflicted. But He was pierced through for our transgressions, He was crushed for our iniquities; the chastening for our well-being fell upon Him, and by His scourging we are healed. All of us like sheep have gone astray, each of us has turned to his own way; but the Lord has caused the iniquity of us all to fall on Him.

Isaiah 53:4-6

Question

Do I live like one who is redeemed by the I Am? Do others look at me and see someone who is different, someone who is forgiving, who lays down his life for others?

Pray

Father, thank You for being stricken, smitten, afflicted, pierced, crushed, chastened, and scourged for my salvation. Thank You for loving me with so great a love that Your only Son died for me.

DAY 60

Full Grace

And the Word became flesh, and dwelt among us, and we beheld His glory, glory as of the only begotten from the Father, full of grace and truth.

John 1:14

Why God Loves Children

Daily family devotions happen at 9:15 in our family. We usually tell a Bible story and talk about what God wants us to do like the people in story we read. Then after the devotion, we pray. One particular evening, our son Edson was praying. His prayers are long and very earnest and precious. As he was praying he said, "And God help me not to be a *caramel* Christian." He continued praying, but I have no idea what he said. All the adults in the room nearly died in silent laughter. Of course, we knew someone had taught him not to be a *carnal* Christian, likely at school. His substitution was delightful. Not wanting to embarrass him, we didn't tell him of his error. After a week of him praying every night that he would not be a caramel Christian, we finally had to tell him he meant a carnal Christian.

It is the sincerity and simplicity of the faith of children that God loves. Children don't see all the failures of life. They just ask God to fix things, and they leave their worries in the hands of the One who is full of grace. For about three months, Edson prayed that he would not be a carnal Christian. Since he doesn't pray that anymore, I think it means God's answered that prayer.

Question

Am I a caramel Christian? Do I put on a sickly sweet outside while inside I am grumbling and greedy and envious of others? Am I genuine or do I put on a fake facade of spirituality?

Pray

Father, give me the faith and sincerity of a child. Fill me full of grace, just as You are full of grace and truth. Give me a clean heart. Cleanse me, make me white as snow. Take from me half-heartedness and unfaithfulness and apathy. Turn my heart from self-pity to see others around me who need Your grace. Made for grace, let me be what You made me to be: grace to others.

DAY 61

Fruit

But the fruit of the Spirit is love, joy, peace, patience, kindness, goodness, faithfulness, gentleness, self-control; against such things there is no law.

Galatians 5:22-23

By This

My children all knew at a very young age how to use the word *fair*. They knew if something wasn't fair. My children (I am blessed with seven) frequently would tell me that my treatment of them or the treatment of them by their siblings wasn't fair. I have noticed that a child's definition of fair is, "I get to have what everyone else has." The more correct definition, "Everyone else gets to have the same as what I have," seems to escape them.

I noticed that I behave the same way with God. I often protest to God the road He has given me. We are all the same way. "Why did You give me this pain, God? Why didn't You share it with someone else?" We are a little more sophisticated than our children, but we are saying the same thing—"God, it's not fair!" We say this when life's burdens seem too hard.

This leads to Galatians 5:22-23. No matter our circumstances, we are called to the fruit of the Spirit. Instead of bitterness, love; instead of resentfulness, joy; instead of demanding what we deserve, peace; instead of instant gratification, patience; instead of religious piety, kindness and goodness; instead of flightiness, faithfulness; instead of pompousness, gentleness; instead of self-gratification, self-control.

Question

Do I protest God's plan because it isn't fair? Do I believe God isn't fair? Am I sealed by the Holy Spirit, walking with the Spirit? Does God see in me quiet, obedient love?

Pray

Father, I cannot bear Your fruit without Your Spirit filling me, transforming me. I ask you to fill me. Let me cry out for You instead of fairness. Let me bear the fruit of Your Spirit in my life.

DAY 62

False Loves

"No one can serve two masters; for either he will hate the one and love the other, or he will be devoted to one and despise the other. You cannot serve God and wealth."

Matthew 6:24

Famished for Food?

Our church has designated a day this week for fasting. We were asked if we are willing to put God first. Are we willing to choose Him over our next meal? The plan is to begin the fast at 7:00 p.m. and end it the next day at 7:00 p.m. Well, this has caused great consternation within our family as we have ten people every night for dinner, and we usually eat around 7:00 p.m. Under this plan, we would miss supper. So as we talked as a family, we began to develop elaborate plans for our last meal. The menu drifted from salmon to steak to macaroni and cheese (suggested by our seven-year-old). We all agreed we needed lots of chocolate cake for desert. Everyone wanted to have their favorite food just before starting our self-imposed fast. Our teenage girls are convinced they will faint if they don't eat. Our college kids are trying to decide if they should feast for twenty-four hours or just eat a little bit leading up to our fasting. All of this has created great conversations, and we have laughed at ourselves and our own anxiety about missing food. At the same time, it has given us pause to realize how dependent we are on our daily bread.

We all have needs and wants in our lives. When those are taken away from us, we begin to realize how much we miss them. We begin to realize that we are placing those things ahead of our Father. Jesus tells us in Matthew chapter 4 that we do not live by bread alone, but by the word of our Father. We do not live by things—neither wealth, power, feasting, fasting, friends, influence nor health gives life. Only "worship the Lord your God, and serve Him only" (Matthew 4:10).

Question

Whom do you serve? Are you balancing two masters? We all have them—gluttony, greed, coveting, etc. Are you ready to give up your next meal because you hunger more for our Father?

Pray

Father, give us this day our daily bread. Give us, above all, Your Kingdom in our lives and let Your name be holy and set apart in our heart. Help us to worship You, our Yahweh Adonai (Lord God). When we are hungry, give us the Word from Your mouth that we may serve You and You only!

DAY 63

Tender Love

I shall make mention of the lovingkindnesses of the Lord, the praises of the Lord, according to all that the Lord has granted us, and the great goodness toward the house of Israel, which He has granted them according to His compassion, and according to the multitude of His lovingkindnesses.

Isaiah 63:7

Perspective

He lay in his hospital bed. His doctor told him the operation had gone well, but his colon cancer had spread. The doctor was vague about how long he had to live. The doctor left him alone in the room—alone with his thoughts, pushing his pain button when the pain grew too much to bear. His wife had died several months ago. Anger grew within him. He had faithfully pastored his flock for forty years. Retired for only six months, he now faced this. How did he deserve this, this painful news of the death awaiting him? "God," he cried out, "why? Is this all you have for me, just an empty death from cancer?"

God answered Him. "I was here in this room waiting for you when you came from surgery. I knew of this day before you were born. You are in my hands, just as you were every day of your life. We will walk through this, and one day you will come home and walk with Me. My grace is sufficient for you."

This pastor, teaching us about God's grace some ten years after he lay in that hospital room, knew firsthand of desperate times. He also knew of God's grace, grace sufficient. As he spoke to us of God's grace, I realized, perhaps for the first time, how much God loves me. All the guilt I carried around as proof that God didn't like me suddenly seemed childish. I realized God had spent eternity planning for my life. He crafted me just perfectly the way He wanted me. He watched my birth, rejoicing to meet me. He planned all the times He would talk with me and help me. He loves me more tenderly than I will ever love my own children. His grace is sufficient for each day, each trial.

Question

Do you know—do you have any idea—of the depth and width and length of His love for you?

Pray

Help me to know Your grace. Help me to know Your tender lovingkindnesses. Help me to speak of the great goodness of God.

DAY 64

Another Reminder

"I have loved you with an everlasting love; therefore I have drawn you with lovingkindness."

Jeremiah 31:3

A Child's Prayer

Tonight during our family devotions, our adopted son from Ethiopia prayed. To understand his prayer, you would have to journey back with us to Ethiopia and see where he is from. He was born into a country desperately poor. His father died from diabetes when our son was five. When he was seven, his mother became sick with malaria. Her two youngest children died from starvation. Knowing that he might be the next to die, she gave him to an orphanage to be adopted. He has been with us in the United States. for over a year. He is learning English so well. He seems happy. Tonight he prayed and asked that God would let his older Ethiopian sister and brothers "not be died."

My wife and I cried quietly as he prayed in a voice so innocent and simple. He just asked for life for his remaining family in Ethiopia. Then he thanked God for his new brothers and sisters and his new parents. We were both a little ashamed at our own petty irritations and frustrations from a long day of work. Somehow, even though he is our son, we forget all that God has given us. We complain because of not having the perfect food or weight or looks or job or gift or car or whatever. Our son's prayer reminded us of what and who is important. We were reminded that God loves us. That truth is so deep we keep learning it every day of our life, and we never scratch the surface.

Question

Do you get caught up in complaining about the petty frustrations of the day, complaining about office politics? Do you forget the goodness of the living God?

Pray

Teach me the depth of Your everlasting love. Draw me with your lovingkindness. Teach me to have the heart of a child.

DAY 65

In Love

Blessed be the God and Father of our Lord Jesus Christ, who has blessed us with every spiritual blessing in the heavenly places in Christ, just as He chose us in Him before the foundation of the world, that we would be holy and blameless before Him. In love He predestined us to adoption as sons through Jesus Christ to Himself, according to the kind intention of His will, to the praise of the glory of His grace, which He freely bestowed on us in the Beloved.

Ephesians 1:3-6

A Love before Time

It was a record night for the number of deliveries by one doctor. By the end of the night, ten children were born, but it was child number eight who is remembered. There was no warning of trouble. The labor had gone well. The doctor rushed in about three in the morning just wanting to finish the delivery safely before rushing off to deliver the last child of the night. The mother pushed, and a beautiful baby girl was born. Except she wasn't so beautiful. Across her upper lip, a deep scar had formed, splitting her precious face into a snarl. As the doctor placed the baby in her mother's arms, the doctor's thoughts raced. How had they missed this on the ultrasound? What would the parents say? The mother, surprise and shock in her voice, could only manage a surprised, "Oh!" That was when they noticed only four fingers on her little hands. There was just a moment of stunned silence. Then the dad stepped to his wife's side and held one of the little hands between his fingers. He felt his daughter grasping him. He said, "Isn't she beautiful? God has given us a beautiful baby girl." After a few moments, he prayed with his wife, thanking God for their new child.

Before time, God planned that child's birth. Before the foundation of the world, He loved that baby girl. So it is with all of us. We aren't born into the world in some random fashion. We are born into this world in His time and at His command. He knits each child just according to His design in the mother's womb. When I think of the love of those parents, I realize that God loves us that much and so much more.

Question

Do you realize how much you mean to God? Do you know that in love He planned your birth, your every moment, your life. He planned to die so that you could know Him. Do you know His love?

Pray

Father, give me this love for those around me. Give me Your love. I am but a clanging symbol without Your Spirit leading me to love. I praise You for the glory of Your grace. I thank You that I am Your beloved.

DAY 66

Goodbyes

Surely goodness and lovingkindness will follow me all the days of my life, and I will dwell in the house of the LORD forever.

Psalm 23:6

Life's End

Part of my job is to tell people that they have cancer. You could never enjoy a job like that, but there is some fulfillment in doing it with kindness and compassion. Having done this for a while, I have seen many people react to being told they have a life-ending illness.

I remember one person in particular. He was young, near my age (old becomes younger every year), and in one week he went from healthy to dying of a kind of cancer for which we have no good treatment. He lived less than a month. He asked me what we could do for him. I gently told him that there was little we could do. He started to shake and shed just a few tears. I stopped what we were doing and prayed with him. As I prayed for him, I wondered how God could think of this as lovingkindness following him all the days of his life. It doesn't feel like lovingkindness. It feels like sadness and pain and death. Since that day, I prayed for him many times. I knew that healing was very unlikely because I know from the book of Job that God has a plan for our lives and each of us must die. Be it young or old, there is an appointed time. I know we are the created vessel and when He calls us home to Him, we will go, no matter what the time or day, no matter the family we leave behind.

One day I know it will be time for me to go to the house of the Lord, forever. When that day comes, I want to be like Paul and say to everyone I love that to die is gain. To die is to go and be with my maker, who is love itself. To die is to begin the greatest dance, to end fear and begin love without end. To live is Christ.

Question

Am I serving Him with all my strength while strength I have? Do I trust Him even when death calls my loved ones? Will I yet trust Him when He calls me home to be with Him?

Pray

Father, restore my soul, lead me beside quiet waters, quell my fears. In life or death, I will cling to You, Father of love.

DAY 67

Abiding

"Just as the Father has loved Me, I have also loved you; abide in My love. If you keep My commandments, you will abide in My love; just as I have kept My Father's commandments and abide in His love. These things I have spoken to you that My joy may be in you, and that your joy may be made full."

John 15:9-11

Abiding by the Rules

The dictionary definition of *abide* means to act in accordance with a rule or a decision. I was climbing Kilimanjaro with my three oldest children several years ago. As we began the climb, I developed a sore throat. No problem. It didn't affect my legs, and I didn't feel sick. However, at the first hut (9,000 feet), I noticed a simple, innocuous sign. DO NOT PROCEED BEYOND THIS POINT IF YOU HAVE AN UPPER RESPIRATORY INFECTION. Now I am a doctor, so I just ignored the sign. I mean it was just a sore throat, what could go wrong? At the second hut (12,000 feet), I showed my fellow climbers the mountain emergency rescue stretcher. Six men guide the stretcher down while a bicycle wheel placed centrally takes the weight of the sick climber. I even laid down on the stretcher to show off. The next morning, I was coughing up yellow junk. The warning sign was long forgotten. We climbed for eight hours to the third hut, Horombo (15,000 feet). Upon arrival, I could not get my breath. I was so cold. I began to realize I was really sick and I could not get enough air. I made the decision to go down and leave my children with the team's guides. It was a tearful farewell.

As I descended with my personal guide, my breathing worsened. I grew weak and finally collapsed, unable to walk or even crawl. My guide left me to go get the stretcher and the six men required to carry me down the mountain. He was gone forever, it seemed. The sun set and the temperature plummeted. I thought I was going to freeze to death. I found out later that my wife, who had stayed at the hotel to take care of our youngest children, was awakened from an evening nap and began praying for me at that exact moment. Finally, as I thought of my wife and children, wondering if I would ever see them again, my guide arrived and bundled me into my sleeping bag. I was placed on the stretcher that I had ridiculed a day earlier and bumped my way down the mountain. The doctor I saw upon my return placed me on antibiotics for pneumonia.

Question

Do you resist abiding in His love? Do you keep His commandments?

Pray

Help me, Father, to obey Your commandments. Let Your joy, Your complete joy fill me.

DAY 68

Rich Mercy, Living Grace

But God, being rich in mercy, because of His great love with which He loved us, even when we were dead in our transgressions, made us alive together with Christ (by grace you have been saved).

Ephesians 2:4-5

Covered by Grace

Do you ever look back at yourself in old pictures? There is a movie of me taken on an old home film movie camera. I was about five with white blond hair. I had a hoe that was about the same size as I was. A team of people were trying to dig a stream for irrigation on our farm. I was helping—or at least I thought I was—as I kept pushing people out of the way. I dug as fast as I could for about thirty seconds. Then I quit and told someone else to take over. The movie always plays back a little fast, so I look ridiculous digging really fast with no change in the ditch. Then I pushed someone else out of the way and did it again.

I wonder about the final judgment in heaven—how we will all stand at the mercy seat, before the Father in His holiness, and be judged. I have always pictured it as if we will watch a movie of our lives and all will be played back. There will be no hiding or disguising our deeds. Imagine how embarrassing and humiliating to see all my greed and lust displayed before heaven. Then I realize that I am saved by grace and I am forgiven. For me and anyone else who is a Christ follower, our movie screen will turn red whenever a part is being played back where we are sinning. The red is the blood of Christ covering our sin. At the end of the story of my life, only the righteous things I have done will be displayed for God to judge. My movie will be sinless, just as yours will be if you are Christ's disciple. To stand before the Father, in all His holiness, and be judged righteous—that is rich mercy and great love. That is a gift I can never repay. May I never be proud of my own righteousness. Let me rather boast of Christ's gift of grace to an utterly unworthy transgressor.

Question

Do others see me as stuck up or prideful of my good deeds? Do others see in me the living grace of Christ which was given as a grace gift?

Pray

Father, thank You for the amazing living grace and rich mercy You have poured into my life. I confess to You I am full of sin and only by Your changing love is my life anything other than darkness and despair. Thank You, Father of light, for loving me.

DAY 69

Unity

Therefore if there is any encouragement in Christ, if there is any consolation of love, if there is any fellowship of the Spirit, if any affection and compassion, make my joy complete by being of the same mind, maintaining the same love, united in spirit, intent on one purpose.

Philippians 2:1-2

Follow Your Kids

It was the end of a family vacation. Our two girls spent the week in ski school, and on the last day we went skiing with them. They begged me to follow them through "Chaos Canyon" where they had skied for classes. Wishing to oblige them and ignoring the obvious name of the route, I followed them into the canyon. My wise wife chose to go around and meet us at the bottom. Why does testosterone always get me into trouble? Things were going fine as I followed Hannah and Emily along the icy, narrow trail. Then, around a sharp corner, right in the middle of the trail, there was a couple facing each other having a throw-down yelling match. For Hannah and Emily it was no problem—they zipped off the trail onto little trails through the woods. I calmly picked out my own trail instead of following my kids. Suddenly, I was on a two-foot wide path and trees were zipping past me at an alarming speed. There was no way to stop. My skis were too long to turn, and it was all I could do to avoid meeting the trees with my face. The end of the forest appeared. That was the good news. The bad news was there was a four-foot drop. It didn't go well. I sprawled onto the trail below, cracking two of my lower right ribs in the process. I lay there unable to take in a breath. It hurt so bad. Worse than the pain were the teenagers who kept jumping over me laughing at the old man who couldn't even jump a little four-foot slope. Finally, I was able to breathe a little. My daughters came back to find me. Emily told me her teacher had told her never to come the way I chose. She couldn't imagine why I would have gone that way. "You should have followed me, Dad!"

I tell this story to remind all of us that at some level, God calls us to stay on the same trails with each other. He calls us to be unified, intent on love, mindful of the same goal. When we choose our own trail, we tend to run into trees or fall off cliffs and break our ribs. God reminds us that love between us through the Spirit brings unity and joy.

Edson L. Knapp

Question

Are there other children of God that I won't share a trail with? Have I pulled out of the race so I don't have to face them? Do I resent that God loves them as much as He loves me?

Pray

Father, give me Your Spirit of unity. Give me Your love for Your children. Give me intention and purpose to follow You. Give me love.

DAY 70

Know Him

For this reason I also suffer these things, but I am not ashamed; for I know whom I have believed and I am convinced that He is able to guard what I have entrusted to Him until that day. Retain the standard of sound words which you have heard from me, in the faith and love which are in Christ Jesus.

2 Timothy 1:12-13

He Is Known

What does it mean that Paul knows whom he believes? It means that Paul is a bondservant of a living God. It means that I am a bondservant of a living God. If you are His then you, too, are a bondservant. This God we serve is not dead. He is not a prophet who died; He is not an idol of gold or possession. He is alive; His name is I Am.

Neema, an orphan in Tanzania, has life today because He lives. She has many friends at the orphanage in Makwale. They have a roof over their heads and a place to sleep because He is a living God. They have shoes and clothes; they have love.

I remember the first time I visited the orphanage when children filled it. I always thought an orphanage was a place where all the children moped around praying that someday a parent or a long-lost relative or someone would come rescue them. This orphanage is so different. The children are filled with love. They are happy and have many friends. Neema said, "At home I did not have food or shoes or a bed or clothes. Now, I have a place to sleep and food."

I have come to realize that our God is a risen God. He is active, accomplishing His will each and every day. It is in Christ that we daily learn from the living God. The more I know Him, the more I see His hand in every part of my life. I am His. I declare, just as Paul, I know whom I have believed and I am persuaded He is able to guard what I have entrusted to Him until that day.

Question

Do you know the living God? Do you see His hand at work? Do you also declare that He is a living God? Do you know that He is love alive, filling each day with light?

Pray

Father, give me the words to tell of Your works in my life. I pray for Your hand upon my life today. Guard me from myself and keep me from sin. Protect me from faithlessness and idle distractions. Let me never be ashamed but rather glory in You.

Edson L. Knapp

DAY 71

What It Comes Down To

But whoever keeps His word, in him the love of God has truly been perfected. By this we know that we are in Him: the one who says he abides in Him ought himself to walk in the same manner as He walked.

1 John 2:5-6

Far from Perfect

We were trying to save money. We bought a haircutting set. It seemed like a good idea. I watched my wife cut our children's bangs and give what seemed like decent haircuts. I finally decided that she could cut my hair. So I sat in the chair. My kids were all gathered around hoping for some major carnage. Things seemed to be going well. Hair was cut in an orderly manner. The clippers clipped and then one sudden movement up the side of my head ended with the words, "Oops!" I was calm, sure that this could be fixed. The mirror spoke otherwise. A gash of near baldness replaced my once handsome sideburn (since I am writing these devotions, the sideburn was handsome). Almost worse, was the jumbled appearance of the entire haircut. It was a testimony to why a license is required to cut hair. That was Saturday night. The next morning my Sunday School class enjoyed my haircut; I mean hair mauling.

It is a great family story (glad I could contribute), and it was also the last haircut my wife has given me. But I tell it here because I think about God's word perfecting us. "Whoever keeps His word, in him the love of God has truly been perfected." As imperfect as my haircut was, as imperfect as we are inside, as far from faithful, as far from grace, as far from holy, God's love perfects us, truly perfects us. By His Spirit, we receive the power to choose obedience, the will to follow His word. From His strength we become followers, disciples. From His love we become truly perfected no matter the appearance of our haircut or the appearance of our heart. Abide in Him, meditate on His word, become transformed in the love of God, His perfect love.

Question

Am I choosing obedience? Am I abiding every day in His word? Do I meditate on His law?

Pray

Father, I am so weak. I choose lawlessness when I know to choose right. I want holiness, but I choose pettiness and gossip. Forgive me, Father. I desire to follow You, to be perfected in You, in Your love. Please change my heart and help me to abide in Your love. Create in me a new heart.

DAY 72

Commended Grace

And now I commend you to God and to the word of His grace, which is able to build you up and to give you the inheritance among all those who are sanctified.

Acts 20:32

Quiet Streams, Thundering Waterfalls

There are times in life that are spent beside quiet streams ... and then a waterfall appears out of nowhere. Our family was on a short-term mission trip to South America. Our team was taken to see the famous Argentinean waterfalls. Little did we realize the stunning falls we were about to experience. We walked through the South American jungle with our guide. Undergrowth mixed with layer after layer of endless shades of green stretched upward above our heads. After twenty minutes, we heard thunder. As we looked upstream, before our eyes we saw hundreds of waterfalls, each over two hundred feet high. As we walked along the edge, we saw Diablo's Throat—a narrow U-shaped, two-hundred-and-fifty-foot deep chasm. The falls pour into the gorge over all three sides with clouds of vapor rising out of the cauldron. As we walked down the steps into the river, the spray misted us and then soaked us. In some areas along the walk, the spray came down like rain. We experienced Iguaçu Falls. Then they put us in big rubber boats with huge outboard motors. We zoomed off into the white water. My wife and I spent our time trying not to let our children be swept overboard. Emily, our youngest daughter, was scared and cold. The thunderous sound of the falls around us drowned out the sound of the engines straining just to keep the boat even with the rushing water. The rumble of the falls shook our bodies with its power.

Paul was encountering his own waterfall. He was leaving the Christians of Ephesus, people whom he had led to the Lord. They were his family. He loved them. He knew that he would never see them again. His words to them were, "now I commend you to God and to the word of His grace."

Question

Do I cling to Him when waterfalls come? Do I cling to Him in the quiet times when the river is full and quiet and safe? Am I sustained by the word of His grace or by the words of myself?

Pray

Father, teach me to rest in Your grace each day, whether in still times or turbulent times. Draw me to Your heart. I commend myself to the word of Your grace.

DAY 73

Love Others

In this is love, not that we loved God, but that He loved us and sent His Son to be the propitiation for our sins. Beloved, if God so loved us, we also ought to love one another.

1 John 4:10-11

His Children

He died for us. We are the children for whom He died. I am always amazed to hear about the mighty movement of God around the world. Returning from a mission trip to Paraguay, we were surprised to discover that almost the entire plane was filled with volunteers returning from South American mission trips. There were small and large groups. The plane was filled with stories of adventures with God. On another trip returning from Tanzania, we met some Korean missionaries—people who were undercover missionaries in a communist country. They were hired to teach Korean to children of Koreans in that country, but that was just their cover. Secretly, they were starting house churches and sharing God's word. There are people of God all over the world giving their lives, some in persecution, loving the people Christ died to save. Others are teaching and discipling His new children. All over this world, He is working. Our daughter Rachel worked with missionaries in France. Their ministry was with the North African Muslims, reaching them as they returned to countries closed to Christianity. They gave out Bibles in the people's own language. The stories go on and on. These are the stories of grace in action.

By the way, I need to note the meaning of "propitiation." It means to appease or pacify or make peace with. In the verse above, it means that God sent His Son to be crucified and die on the cross so He could have peace with us; God's demand for justice was appeased by Christ's death.

I know God's love by His sacrifice for me. By His grace, there are others that He died for who are waiting for me to share the good news with them. Others who know Him are waiting for me to share with them the lessons I have learned.

Question

What is my ministry? Is He using me for His church, for those who don't know Him? Am I willing to be interrupted for His work?

Pray

Father, I want to be obedient to Your will. I want to share with others the love You gave to me. Teach me to have time for others. Show me how to love like You. Give me grace to be like You for others.

DAY 74

By Grace Adopted

He chose us in Him before the foundation of the world, that we should be holy and blameless before Him. In love He predestined us to adoption as sons through Jesus Christ to Himself, according to the kind intention of His will.

Ephesians 1:4-5

In Love

Our family adopted our seventh child. He is from Ethiopia, and he has become one of us, both legally and in our hearts. We think of him as ours just as we think of our other children. He has a wonderful sense of humor, and he loves to make us laugh. This story is the prequel of the adoption. We felt complete as parents and as a family. Six children, busy careers as two doctors, and our plate was full. Completely unaware of what was coming, we met a couple who was considering adopting a child. My wife, wanting to help them, researched adoptions from Ethiopia. We even offered to help them with the expenses and the process. After some deliberation, they decided they just didn't feel called to pursue a child. I remember the night when they left our house and we went upstairs. All the papers were on our bed. It was somehow a little deflating. That was when my wife announced that she felt God had led us through the whole process so that we would adopt a child. I was astounded (an understatement). We were finished with diapers and strollers, and we were full of children. Our house never has a dull moment, and often I find myself trying to find a quiet spot. Yet, her words resounded in my heart. A child, orphaned and starving, could be given a place with our family. Suddenly the decision was made. Our hearts leapt forward and we entered the process with abandon. One day we came upon a list of older orphans (six or seven years of age). We found ourselves drawn to the description of one who had the same birth date as my wife. The day we received his picture, we fell in love with him. Over the years since that day, God has shown us he chose that child to be a part of our family. As blessed as our seventh child is to have us, we are more blessed to have him as our son.

When I think with how much joy we anticipated our adopted son, I realize why God sent His Son to die for us so that He could adopt us into His family. When we were born, He rejoiced to meet us. He has spent eternity planning for us, and now those plans are finally here. His heart leaps for joy as each of us accepts His grace and are adopted into His family. It is a love beyond theology, beyond understanding, beyond our heart's own love. We are each adopted by grace.

Question

Am I walking blameless before Him? Am I a joy to grace?

Pray

Father, thank You for my adoption. The cost You paid for me to be Your child is beyond comprehension. Let me be a joy to You today! I bless Your name. I bow in humility for the grace You have shown to me.

DAY 75

Hope

Beloved, now we are children of God, and it has not appeared as yet what we will be. We know that when He appears, we will be like Him, because we will see Him just as He is. And everyone who has this hope fixed on Him purifies himself, just as He is pure.

1 John 3:2-3

Don't Know

It was time to meet our seventh child. I remember the green grass, worn down by children playing. Walls protected the orphanage. Monkey bars and a slide and swing set adorned the small outdoor area. My wife and I had looked at his picture thousands of times. Now, getting ready to see him for the first time, we were filled with excitement and tension. He was sitting with his friends in a classroom. Their teacher was leading them in rote recitation of the ABCs. The social worker brought him out of the small room. He recognized us from the pictures that we had sent him. He ran to us and in very broken English called us mom and dad. He hugged us and said, "I love you." My wife was crying. It was an unreal experience. We played soccer in the courtyard. We played on the swings. He took us to his room where he slept with the other orphans. It was the first time we met our son. What a day of joy and apprehension. What a day of excitement.

Going through that experience makes me wonder what it will be like when we see God our Father face to face. We, His children, seeing Him as He appears. How great a meeting, how great a celebration. How great a love. The group Mercy Me has a song about that time, called "I Can Only Imagine." The lyrics express wonder at whether we will be able to speak at all on that day. I think all of us who know Him, long for that day when we will meet our Father and tell Him of our love for Him. That will be a day when we are pure before Him, just as He is pure. That will be a day when we will rejoice. That will be a day when we will see Him just as He is. It will be a day of joy beyond imagining.

Question

Am I ready to meet God? Am I walking after Him? Am I purifying myself just as He is pure?

Pray

Father, as I follow Your will here on Earth, I ask for Your holiness in my life. I ask for Your kingdom here in me, in my home, in my church, and in my community. I ask for Your will to be done. I ask for Your strength, because my strength is so small.

DAY 76

Children

See how great a love the Father has bestowed upon us, that we would be called children of God; and such we are. For this reason the world does not know us, because it did not know Him.

1 John 3:1

A Special Christmas

We didn't have a Christmas tree. It was hot. There weren't many presents—we had only one small present for each of our children. But it was to be our children's favorite Christmas. We were in Makwale, Tanzania, and I had taken my family to have Christmas with the orphans in Makwale. Dinner was rice and beans and chicken. One Coke for each orphan. The ladies of the church had prepared huge tubs of food. Each child piled a plate high with rice and gravy with a little meat and beans. Neema and Eva sat with us at the wooden tables. They were four and five years old. Our children, who pick at their food, were amazed as those little girls put away a massive plate of rice. Neema even ate part of Emily's meal. Their little bellies were so full. Their big, brown eyes were full of happiness. After dinner, we gave out presents to every child. It was so much fun. One child got a pair of sunglasses and ran all over the courtyard demonstrating his new coolness. The younger children wandered around sucking on candy and watching the older kids running and playing with their new gifts. Instead of a Christmas tree, we put lights around a cross.

How great a love there was that day. How special it was to watch the children have a day filled with love. It is to this day our children's favorite Christmas.

I think of God's love for us, that he would call us His children. I think He enjoyed that Christmas Day as much as we did. He has plans for good for each one of us.

Question

Am I taking my Father for granted? Am I sharing His great love with widows and orphans?

Pray

Father, thank You for Your love, Your great love of me. Forgive me when I love less, care less, and help less than You made me to love. Help me to love others as myself—help me to love them as You love them.

DAY 77

Rich Grace

To the praise of the glory of His grace, which He freely bestowed on us in the Beloved. In Him we have redemption through His blood, the forgiveness of our trespasses, according to the riches of His grace.

Ephesians 1:6-7

Poor in Spirit

Who needs grace? In the bottom of the second inning, our team was in need of help. Our two youngest, ages seven and eight, were on a Little League team, the Richlands Astros. At this age, the pitching is done by a pitching machine placed on the pitching mound. The score was Astros 2, Cardinals 5. Our coach called the players together, exhorting them that we needed some hits if we hoped to catch up and win the game. There is something so endearing watching those little boys in their uniforms gathered around their coach and hanging on every word. The coach delivered his pep talk and the first batter was up. He struck out. Next was our eight-year-old son. He was desperate for a hit. He is so competitive. We watched him step up to the plate. The ball sailed toward him. A fast, powerful swing caught only air. Strike one! He stepped out of the box. Stretching, he swung the bat, loosening himself, shrugging off the miss. Again he stepped to the plate. The parents leaned in while the kids in the dugout started yelling his name. Strike two! Another stretch, another shrug followed by more cheering. Strike three. Crestfallen, he returned to the dugout. They lost the game. On the way to the car, he couldn't contain himself, he broke into sobs. I picked him up and laid his head on my shoulder so others wouldn't see his tears.

We went to get some ice cream and that cheered him up. Soon he was chasing his brother around the restaurant, laughing and happy again. I thought about how simple grace is for a child. Just comfort, encouraging words, and some ice cream, and he was right as rain. Why can't we receive God's grace so freely? I also realized all of us need grace. We have all struck out, missing the ball. All of us fail before the holiness of God. We daily, urgently need His grace, His freely given grace which He pours out on His children according to their needs.

Question

Am I walking in His grace today? Am I seeking the riches of His grace or the poverty of my own desires and self-will?

Pray

Father, thank You for saving me through Your grace. I pray for my heart to be opened to all that Your grace is for me today. I praise You for the glory of Your grace.

DAY 78

Small Eyes

Therefore do not be ashamed of the testimony of our Lord or of me His prisoner, but join with me in suffering for the gospel according to the power of God, who has saved us and called us with a holy calling, not according to our works, but according to His own purpose and grace which was granted us in Christ Jesus from all eternity.

2 Timothy 1:8-9

Where Am I Going?

Four of us decided to climb the Livingstone Mountains near our Matema guest house. We were staying there during our three-week mission trip to Tanzania. The mountains beckoned us, inviting us to climb out of the valley. A driver dropped us off next to a small path. In the early morning darkness, we set out toward the mountain. After several farms, we reached the base of the mountain and the end of any discernible path. We set out into the brush, weaving between elephant grass and trees. Within minutes we were hot and sweaty. The grass cut our arms and the sweat stung. I was designated as the leader because I had climbed here before. It was no advantage. As I walked across the elephant grass I had pushed beneath my feet, the ground gave way and I fell into what seemed like a cave. Unhurt, except for pride, I looked around with my flashlight and realized I was not in a cave but under a small tree. The grass had grown over the tree, leaving a small hut-like structure in which I stood. All around me was a wall of grass and leaves and cob webs with spiders gazing back at me.

We pushed through the wall of leaves and grass toward the mountain. We fought through more grass and "huts." Several hours later, as the sun rose behind us, we looked over the plain beneath us. It was beautiful. The lake lay to the south and we could see the whole district laid out like a jeweled carpet.

I find myself in the weeds of life so often. I feel trapped by finances and illness and circumstances. Spiders look at me, waiting to pounce if I become trapped in their webs. God's plan of grace is granted us from an eternal perspective. From His view, the plan for our lives is laid out. There is no fear, only beauty and fulfillment and love. His eyes are not as small as mine. He sees His purpose where I see elephant grass and weeds and spiders.

Question

Do I trust in God's plan or my eyes?

Pray

Father, grant me the peace of knowing You have grace granted me from all eternity. Work Your purpose in my life and forgive me when I fail to trust You. Help me to see with Your big eyes instead of my small eyes which see only fear at every turn.

DAY 79

Love for a Son

Know therefore that the LORD your God, He is God, the faithful God, who keeps His covenant and His lovingkindness to a thousandth generation with those who love Him and keep His commandments.

Deuteronomy 7:9

A Father's Love

Recently, my son Matthew wrote me a letter of gratitude. It was one of those letters written by a young man who, having just finished college, wants to express his gratitude to his parents. It was a two-page letter and it said many of the things you would expect. There was the admission that we had been right all along (of course). More gratifying, however, he thanked us for spending time investing in his life. He noticed that we spent time loving him and being kind to him. It was a wonderful letter for a parent to read.

When I look at God my Father, I realize I need to write Him the same letter. How many times has He kept me from danger? How many times have His commandments protected me? How much I have benefited from His love and kindness to me, His child.

Love and Kindness

It's right there in the Ten Commandments (see Exodus 20:6). It is almost God's commandment to Himself. It is His expression of love for His children. He will show love and kindness to His children. You might ask why He requires us to love and obey Him in order for Him to express His love and kindness to us. The answer is that is how we are made. It is our design. He knows it is only as we walk after Him in obedience that we will become what He made us to be. We cannot receive His love and kindness if we walk in disobedience. We cannot follow the adventure in life He prepared for us if we follow our own selfish way. He grieves over us when we forget Him, when we forget our first love.

Question

Do you know that God loves you and wants to pour out His kindness on you? Do you want that relationship with your Creator? Do you want to know the love that the King of Kings has for you?

Pray

Forgive me, Father, for loving myself more than You. I have failed to love others as You love them. I have failed to obey You. I want to know the adventure You have for me. Help me to love You and obey You today. Help me to love my family, my friends, and anyone You bring across my path today.

DAY 80

Love the Lord Our God

"Hear, O Israel! The LORD is our God, the LORD is one! "And you shall love the LORD your God with all your heart and with all your soul and with all your might."

Deuteronomy 6:4-5

A Great Event

My wife called me with unexpected, good news. We scrambled to get airline tickets and receive time off from work. We found ourselves suddenly on Ethiopian Airways flying to Addis Ababa. As the plane took off from Washington, DC, she asked me if I believed this was really happening. I said I couldn't believe it was true. Eighteen hours later, we were lying in bed in a small room on the fifth floor in a quiet neighborhood in Addis. Unable to sleep, I thought about what was to happen the next day. Such a long journey to come down to this.

Morning broke with rooster's crowing. Horns beeped, Amharic voices floated over the noise. As the sunlight illuminated the city, we rose and dressed, nervous about what we were wearing. Would he think we were too old? Would he be disappointed in us? My heart was so anxious. We boarded a bus and rode to the orphanage. As we walked the last few steps, the social worker told us we would be the first parents in our group to meet our child, a seven-year-old Ethiopian boy.

He came running out of the classroom when they told him we were there. We recognized him immediately from his picture we had seen months earlier. All I felt when I saw him was a rush of love, as if he were my long-lost child, now found.

Hear! Hear, my heart, that God made me for love. He made me to love and to be loved. Every part of who I am is made to love God. He adopted me as His son. He knew my weaknesses, my sin, my guilt—and yet He died on a cross so that I could know His love. Hear! Hear, my heart, of the love of the God of all, the I AM, knowing me, His child.

Question

Do I love God with all my heart, with all my soul, and with all my might—this God who adopted me from death row, died on a cross to pay my debt? This God calls me His son.

Pray

Father, I thank You for loving me. I thank You for adopting me. I praise You for teaching me to love. I hear Your command to love You. Unfetter my heart that I might love You more than yesterday.

CPSIA information can be obtained at www.ICGtesting.com
Printed in the USA
LVOW12s2307310713

345427LV00005B/6/P